CASCADIA CLASH

SOUNDERS VERSUS TIMBERS

GEOFFREY C. ARNOLD

• FOREWORD by KASEY KELLER • FOREWORD by MLS COMMISSIONER DON GARBER •

Charleston THE History PRESS London

Published by The History Press
Charleston, SC 29403
www.historypress.net

Cover design by Natasha Walsh.

Front cover, top left: Courtesy of the Seattle Sounders; *top right:* Courtesy of the Portland Timbers; *bottom:* Anatoliy Lukich. *Back cover, top:* Geoffrey C. Arnold; *bottom:* Courtesy of the Portland Timbers.

Seattle Sounders and Portland Timbers properties courtesy of Major League Soccer, LLC.

MLS, Seattle Sounders and Portland Timbers do not endorse views and opinions published on these pages and accept no responsibility for them. Views and opinions are strictly those of the author, and comments or questions regarding the content should be sent directly to the author.

First published 2013

Manufactured in the United States

ISBN 978.1.60949.642.5

Library of Congress CIP data applied for.

CONTENTS

FOREWORD

I t's a cliché, but sometimes you simply cannot believe something until you
see it.

So, on the rainy April evening I took Jon Miller, the president of
programming for NBC Sports and the NBC Sports Network, to Jeld-Wen
Field for the Portland Timbers' opening game of the 2011 Major League
Soccer season, I knew any words I might use to describe to Jon what he was
about to witness would not do it justice.

He had to see it, hear it and feel it for himself. He had to see the capacity
crowd standing on their feet, all dressed in forest green, waving their
enormous flags as the teams warmed up. He had to hear the Timbers Army
lead the crowd of twenty-two thousand in full voice in the singing "The Star-
Spangled Banner." He had to feel the whole place rumble when the Timbers
scored their first goal. And he had to witness one of the most unique fan-
inspired traditions in all of sports, Portland mascot Timber Joey firing up
his chain saw to cut off a section of log and hold it aloft for the fans to see.

When Jon had seen it all, this veteran sports executive who'd been to all
of our country's biggest sporting events, said, "I've never seen anything like
this. I'm blown away."

And yet I was thinking, "If he thinks this atmosphere was special, wait
until he sees what it looks like when the Seattle Sounders are in town. Or
when Portland visits Seattle."

Soccer in the Pacific Northwest is rich in tradition and long on history. The
rivalry between the region's two largest cities, Seattle and Portland, and their

teams, the Sounders and the Timbers, dates back to the '70s. Even during the years following the demise of the North American Soccer League, these two clubs found a way to keep the rivalry flowing, putting together teams at various levels to go head-to-head. It was just a matter of time before Seattle and Portland made their way to Major League Soccer.

Going back to the inception of MLS in 1996, a team for Seattle was in the works. When the proposal for the NFL Seahawks' new downtown stadium was on the table in the late '90s, it was the city's soccer fans who helped convince the politicians to make the stadium now known as Century Link Field a reality. Our league's first commissioner, Doug Logan, promised the soccer fans of the Emerald City, "If you build it, an MLS team will come." And it did.

Credit the "dream team" ownership group, led by Hollywood producer Joe Roth, local entrepreneur Adrian Hanauer and television star and comedian Drew Carey, for not only getting the deal done but also for making sure that when the Sounders FC became a part of MLS in 2009, their fans would be fully prepared to show their passion for the game.

Rituals like the March to the Match through the streets of Seattle, replete with the Sounders' own marching band, and the Golden Scarf, which is presented before each game to someone who represents the team or the community in a special way, are now known worldwide. When the Golden Scarf is raised before each Sounders game and nearly forty thousand Sounders fans follow suit by raising their own scarves, even the most hardened sports fan cannot help but get chills.

The formation of an MLS team in Portland began in 2007, when Merritt Paulson and his father, former United States Treasury secretary Hank Paulson, began working with the City of Portland on a renovation of Civic Stadium, an old minor-league baseball stadium, into a soccer venue. The fans of the Rose City could hardly contain their excitement when it was announced the Timbers would be joining MLS in 2011. Season tickets quickly sold out, and the club had a "season ticket waiting list" five thousand names long.

All that was left was for the Sounders and Timbers to meet on the field, which they did for the first time as a part of MLS on May 14, 2011, in front of 36,593 fans—including 500 members of the Timbers Army—at CenturyLink Field. Songs rang out from both sides. Fans stood throughout the night. The game ended in a 1–1 draw. A perfect result in many ways because in a soccer rivalry like this, many scores will be settled down the road.

But don't let me tell you the story of the rivalry that's now part of the Cascadia Cup with their neighbors to the north, the Vancouver Whitecaps. Please allow Geoffrey C. Arnold to share this with you, from his exhaustive research and interviews to his eyewitness accounts. It's a story that will touch all those who love soccer, not just those with ties to the Pacific Northwest, the Sounders or the Timbers.

And when you're finished with the book, do yourself one more favor. Try to score a ticket to a game in Seattle or Portland. You won't believe it until you see it.

Don Garber, MLS commissioner

FOREWORD

Rivalries are the cornerstone of sports. Every league around the world has rivalries. Some date back centuries and others are forming right in front of our eyes. These rivalries form for many different reasons. Some of the oldest clubs in Europe have families that have been rivals for generations. Rivalries can be based on factors such as religion, geography, social class or family tradition, just to name a few.

One example is the Celtic-Rangers rivalry in Glasgow, Scotland. The supporters are separated by one of the most fundamental motivators: religion. Celtic supporters are primarily Catholics, while Protestants are the primary supporters of Rangers.

In England, the proximity of the teams is what drives and strengthens the rivalries. The rivalries in England aren't limited to the London teams. For example, take the Liverpool-Everton rivalry, where the clubs are separated by a distance of about one mile. A river separates the stadiums of rivals Nottingham Forest and Notts County. One of the big rivalry games that I played in was Millwall versus West Ham in England. This rivalry was started by London dockworkers at the shipyards on either side of the River Thames in the nineteenth century.

While I was playing in Germany, I got myself into trouble when I was playing for Borussia Monchengladbach in the German Bundesliga. We had just defeated our biggest rival, FC Koln, 2–1 at home. I was handed a microphone and proceeded to proudly sing an anti-Koln song. Our supporters joined in, and we thoroughly enjoyed the occasion. We were having a great time, but Wolfgang Overath, the FC Koln president who attended the game, was not amused. The offended Overath reported the incident to the German Football Association, and I was fined €3,000 (about $3,800) for bringing the game into "disrepute." Nonetheless, the incident helped increase the intensity of the rivalry between the two clubs.

Rivalries are common in Europe, but a number of factors have prevented the formation and development of significant soccer rivalries in the United States. One of the biggest factors is the long distances between teams in Major League Soccer (MLS). The relatively short distance between clubs in many European leagues allows supporters to easily travel to away games. In contrast, hundreds—even thousands—of miles separate some MLS teams, making it difficult for supporter groups to attend away games, removing an important element in creating rivalries.

Many major professional sports leagues in the United States share multiple teams in the same city, creating natural rivalries. Some examples are the NFL's New York Giants and Jets and the NBA's Los Angeles Lakers and Clippers.

Another big problem is the relatively young—seventeen years, at this writing—age of the league. With so many professional soccer teams and leagues over the years folding, reforming and folding again, fans haven't been able to develop a lasting loyalty to a certain league or team in the United States compared to the generations of fans who support some teams that have been in existence for more than a century in Europe.

There is one particular rivalry that does possess the important elements— proximity, a long history (at least for U.S. soccer) and passionate fan support—that have made it the biggest rivalry match in the United States: Seattle versus Portland.

What has made the Sounders-Timbers derby the biggest rivalry in American soccer? I think a few things have contributed.

The distance between the two cities is about 180 miles, an easy three-hour drive north or south on Interstate 5 for supporters. When supporters are able to attend an away game, those supporters add an important and enthusiastic element to a rivalry game.

The history between these two teams dates back to 1975, when they competed in the old North American Soccer League. Both franchises have struggled to remain in existence over the years, but now, after decades of playing each other in the lower divisions of the sport that started, maintained and grew the rivalry, both teams have reached the highest level of professional soccer in the United States: Major League Soccer. These two franchises are helping push MLS to unprecedented levels of commercial and popular success that soccer has not seen since the Pelé-driven heyday of the NASL in the mid-1970s.

The single biggest reason why Sounders-Timbers is the best soccer rivalry in the United States? The fans! The supporter groups of each club simply refused to let the history die the death of so many different incarnations of these two storied franchises. The largest of these groups are the Emerald City Supporters (or ECS) in Seattle, and in Portland, there is the Timbers Army, with their chainsaw-wielding mascot "Timber Joey," the successor to the original mascot, "Timber Jim."

I began my playing career as a member of the semiprofessional incarnation of the Timbers one summer while attending the University of Portland in 1989. Now fast-forward nineteen years later to signing with the Sounders after a seventeen-year playing career in Europe.

I want to thank the fans in Seattle and Portland for keeping the dream alive so that one day our sport could rise to the levels that we dreamed it could achieve in this country. Your dedication, perseverance and passion have truly set the standard for soccer not only in the Pacific Northwest but also across the country.

Read and enjoy Geoffrey C. Arnold's book detailing this great rivalry. Players, coaches, games, traditions, tifos and much more are included in his book. I've had the rare privilege of being a player on both sides, and I'm proud to be given the opportunity to share with you some experiences on this subject.

Kasey Keller

ACKNOWLEDGEMENTS

I sincerely thank all the individuals I interviewed for the book. Your contributions are what made this book possible.

I would like to thank the Portland Timbers and Seattle Sounders, whose support throughout this project was critical. The Sounders: Frank McDonald, Jeff Garza and Mike Ferris. The Timbers: Marc Kostic and Chris Metz. I also thank Steve Clare, editor of *Prost Amerika*; Pete Fewing; and *Oregonian* colleague Shawn Levy.

My sincere thanks to Aubrie Koenig at The History Press for guiding me through the publishing process by calmly answering all my questions.

Lastly, I want to thank my family—my wife, Susanna, and my son, Austin, and daughter, Janelle. I could not have completed this project without your patience, inspiration and encouragement.

I'm sure I've missed some names. My apologies to anyone I failed to mention.

INTRODUCTION

From the days when 8,131—or 6,913, depending on who was counting—fans watched the first game of the rivalry in the North American Soccer League in 1975 to the 36,593 fans who attended the first Major League Soccer regular season game in 2011, the Seattle-Portland soccer rivalry is unlike any other in the United States.

It is also the best soccer rivalry in the United States and one of the best in the world. The rivalry, with its history, proximity and similarities of each city, is a competition that ranks among the most heated soccer derbies in the world.

Many factors have influenced the rivalry to transform it into what it is today. Start with the two cities located in the same Pacific Northwest region of the United States, separated by just 180 miles. Throw in a long-held perception of sibling rivalry, with a big brother (Seattle)/little brother (Portland) inferiority complex. In addition, a decades-long rivalry has existed in other sports between the two cities.

Perhaps the sports rivalry between the two cities started when the Portland Rosebuds and the (Seattle) Metropolitans started mixing it up during minor-league games in the Pacific Coast Hockey Association dating back to 1915. It's a rivalry that has carried over into an occasionally ugly and bloody rivalry between the Portland Winter Hawks and Seattle Thunderbirds' minor-league hockey clashes. The Seattle SuperSonics and Portland Trail Blazers battled each other for thirty-eight years before the Sonics relocated to Oklahoma City in 2008.

On the field, tensions usually rise to heightened levels when the same players face one another numerous times over the years. Some of the players have switched allegiances, and others were born and raised in one city only to play for the enemy.

The Sounders and Timbers players are escorted onto the field by youngsters prior to the game at Portland's Jeld-Wen Field, June 24, 2012. *Anatoliy Lukich.*

And then there are the fans, some of the most passionate—sometimes unruly—in the world. Singing and chanting fans that toss streamers, ignite smoke bombs and light flares, scream insults and obscenities at the opposition and, yes, even resort to European-style fisticuffs on occasion.

Each team's venues have produced another source of energy that fuels the rivalry. Seattle's CenturyLink Field is a 67,000-seat behemoth originally built for the city's National Football League Seattle Seahawks. The bigness (capacity is 38,500 for Sounders games) has helped create an attendance and fan-supported juggernaut that is the envy of Major League Soccer.

Portland's home stadium possesses an intimacy that was enhanced after a recent renovation has transformed the stadium into a soccer-specific stadium in 2011. The new design and configuration has increased the influence of the Timbers Army, the most intimidating supporter group in professional soccer in the United States.

The Seattle-Portland rivalry dates back nearly four decades to 1975. Though the history pales in comparison to many European soccer rivalries—the Manchester United–Manchester City derby started in 1894—the Sounders-Timbers competition is old enough to generate intense reactions from different soccer fans in the Northwest and beyond.

The seeds of the rivalry were planted in January 1975, when the rapidly expanding NASL continued its western expansion by awarding a franchise to Portland. Seattle had joined the league in 1974, and the Sounders had already produced a solid inaugural season with impressive attendance.

Chapter 1
THE BEGINNINGS

Walt Daggatt didn't plan to start a professional soccer club; his original dream was to help bring NFL football to the Northwest. The Portland-born Daggatt (he graduated from Grant High School in Northeast Portland) traveled to Dallas, Texas, in an attempt to convince NFL owners to award a franchise to the city of Seattle. During his trip, Daggatt bumped into Lamar Hunt, the owner of the NFL's Kansas City Chiefs.

Hunt, a huge soccer fan, was also a co-founder of the NASL and owner of the NASL's Dallas Tornado (Hunt would eventually be the driving force behind the creation of Major League Soccer). Hunt, who died in 2006, was such an avid supporter of soccer in the United States that the trophy for the U.S. Open Cup championship, the nation's annual tournament, is named after him.

The conversation between Daggatt and Hunt was supposed to focus on football, American style, but the chat steered toward futbol, the world game.

"He got my dad inspired about the NASL," said Russ Daggatt, one of Walt Daggatt's three sons.

Daggatt came away from the talk intrigued by soccer, but he still wanted football. However, Daggatt was partnering with some very high rollers in the Seattle business community.

"We had a high-powered group of the old establishment in Seattle that was bringing in the NFL team, but my dad wasn't quite in the same financial league as those guys," Russ Daggatt said. "He couldn't afford to put up the money to be part of the NFL. Instead, he put together his own partnership for a soccer team."

Walt Daggatt (middle, with ball) traveled to Texas in search of an NFL franchise, but he returned to Seattle with an NASL franchise. The Sounders started play in 1974. *From 1976 Sounders Yearbook, courtesy of Russ Daggatt.*

Daggatt, the managing general partner of the franchise, assembled a group of prospective owners that included Lloyd Nordstrom, Lamont Bean, Lynn Himmelman, Howard Wright, David Skinner and Herman Sarkowsky. The NASL awarded Seattle a franchise to begin play in 1974, during an era of unprecedented growth within the NASL. The league, which had nine clubs in 1973, added Seattle and seven other clubs—including Vancouver— in 1974.

Daggatt didn't use the existing business model for NASL teams, which had placed an emphasis on marketing to specific ethnic groups in cities, particularly on the East Coast. Many of the businessmen and entrepreneurs running teams figured that English, Scottish, Germans, Italians and other ethnic groups living in the United States, hungry for soccer, would support the local clubs.

What some of the NASL owners didn't understand was the finicky nature of those European fans. Those sophisticated fans expected to see first-class soccer and quickly recognized bad soccer when they saw it. Another mistake by some owners was not realizing those fans would support players who were fellow countrymen instead of some disparate group of footballers comprising a club. And those fans would first support clubs playing back in their home countries before backing a club in which they had little or no connection.

"Up to that time, the NASL teams had focused on the ethnic markets. In Rochester [New York], it was the Italian market. In Los Angeles, it was the Hispanic community," Russ Daggatt said. "There tended to be this ethnic focus in the league."

Daggatt implemented a strategy of marketing the club to the general community, pitching the game to suburban families, specifically middle-class families. The decision coincided with the upsurge in popularity of youth soccer in the United States.

"Seattle was the first team in the NASL that took kind of a different approach to soccer. My dad was one of the first ones to believe that the future of soccer was in the suburbs," Daggatt said. "He said, 'We're going to market to the suburbs and build an American team and really tie the team to youth soccer.'" With the growth of the NASL, as well as youth and adult recreational soccer, Daggatt's focus on youth soccer and families was a shrewd one.

"I don't think Walt knew a lot about soccer, but he knew how to deal with people in the right manner," said Jimmy Gabriel, who played for the Sounders from 1974 to 1976 and coached the team from 1977 through 1979. "Walt did a great job of getting the team to connect with the community. The city really responded."

The Sounders didn't qualify for the playoffs in 1974, but the club averaged 13,434 fans each home game, a success by any criteria at the time.

Seattle players wave and acknowledge the support of their fans after a game in 1975. *Sounders 1976 Yearbook, courtesy of Russ Daggatt.*

"We played in a small stadium, and most of our games were sold out," said John Best, who was the Sounders' first coach in 1974. "You basically had to buy a ticket a couple of weeks ahead of the game if you were going to go to a game."

Some fans couldn't get a ticket to watch the game inside Memorial Stadium, but they didn't give up. A few even used Seattle's most famous landmark to watch.

"People would buy tickets and go into the Space Needle and look down at the game from there," said Bernie Fagan, a defender on the 1974 team.

The league took notice. The following year, the league, giddy after Brazilian superstar Pelé signed a three-year deal with the New York Cosmos, expanded again by awarding franchises to Portland and four other cities in 1975.

———•———

Don Paul had trained one eye north to Seattle during the Sounders' inaugural NASL season while preparing to apply for an expansion franchise in Portland. Paul figured if professional soccer could succeed in Seattle, success was nearly a slam-dunk in Portland.

"I called Seattle…to ask them how things were coming along for the 1975 season," Paul told the *Portland Oregonian* on April 8, 1975. "And they told me that they have already sold 5,480 season tickets. This is only their second year of professional soccer and it puts them in the black."

Paul didn't know much about soccer when he pitched the idea to some investors. What Paul did know was how to package, promote and sell a product.

"Don was like Barnum and Bailey. He was a great promoter," said Mick Hoban, a defender on the 1975 Timbers team. "I always have to laugh and smile, because he seemed like he was always selling the team."

Paul was among the thirty-nine stockholders to put up the $350,000 expansion fee for the Timbers to join the NASL. The stockholders elected a board of directors, which included John Gilbertson, Keith Williams, Ken Poreman and Fritz Johnson.

Always fit, tanned and wearing a smile as big as his NFL championship rings—he was a member of the Cleveland Browns NFL championship teams in 1954 and 1955—Paul was a larger-than-life figure in Portland.

"He always seemed to wear these bright colored suits. It was like right out of [the television series] *Starsky and Hutch*," said Jimmy Kelly, a midfielder who played for the Timbers in 1975–76 and 1981. "He was a very confident man who loved the team. Knowing his history as a championship football player, you just had this belief that he could make this work."

Paul—like Daggatt—had wanted an NFL franchise. But Seattle had the inside track for the NFL franchise. Paul, wanting to take advantage of the latest sports fad and seeing the success in Seattle, turned his attention to soccer.

Taking a page out of the Sounders' marketing playbook, Paul aggressively pushed soccer toward the city's youth. At the time, Portland had an estimated 3,500 children registered in soccer programs and the numbers were increasing.

"I know my dad considered the Timbers and the (Minnesota) Kicks as being kind of kindred spirits in terms of where they saw the future of soccer," Russ Daggatt said. "They kind of worked together—they compared notes to see what worked. Portland and Seattle had a spirited rivalry on the field, but off the field from a business standpoint, they were partners."

The owners recognized that the kids may know how to play soccer and understand the game, but they wouldn't be the ones buying tickets to Timbers games. Adults didn't have a clue about the game. But once again, the entrepreneurial Paul had a plan. Instead of going out and trying to explain the rules, intricacies and nuances of soccer himself, Paul just sold the product and its advantages.

"He had the cache of being an NFL star, and he used that to his advantage," Hoban said. "People were always willing to listen to him. He spoke so positively about the Timbers and soccer and the league, and people at least gave it credibility because it was coming from Don Paul."

Don Paul was the driving force behind the NASL awarding a franchise to the city of Portland in 1975. *Photo courtesy of the* Oregonian.

Hoban and Brian Godfrey were the first Portland players to arrive in town, and they were tasked with educating people about the game.

"When I came, they sort of latched on to me and said, 'Oh great. We've got a player. Now you can share some of this load,'" Hoban said. "I literally went to the Kiwanis and Rotary Clubs, anywhere and everywhere. I was made available to the front office, and I was scheduled typically two or three times a day to go somewhere and speak to various groups."

The city welcomed the "new" guys with open arms.

"People would invite us into their homes. You would go to the home and maybe the whole block or a cul-de-sac would be involved," Kelly said. "They knew the Timbers were coming over, and the kids would be very excited."

Hoban was soon joined by other players who made the trip from England, with many of them arriving in Portland on the same flight. The new players quickly learned that playing a sport virtually unknown in an unfamiliar city would require all of them to do some work in promoting the new club.

The public relations requirement was new for many of the players. There was never a need to promote a club or educate the public about soccer in England.

"People like Willie Anderson, Ray Martin and Brian Godfrey, those guys had established themselves as senior players in England. They might do a speaking engagement or a clinic two or three times a year," Hoban said. "There wasn't a vibrant community relations program in those days back in England. So typically, those type of players might visit a hospital during the Christmas season once or twice a year.

"When they came to the States, the expectation was they would do something in the community once or twice a week. Or in certain situations, once or twice a day."

CREATING THE NICKNAMES

The Timbers were close to being called the Pioneers. Not the groundbreaking pioneers of the soccer craze in the city, but the Portland "Pioneers" of the NASL. During a contest to name the new soccer club in early 1975, area residents submitted more than three thousand entries to the Timbers' office. The most popular name? Pioneers.

"There were 157 entries of Pioneers," Paul told the *Oregonian* on March 9, 1975. But that name had been taken by the athletic teams of Lewis and

Portland coach Vic Crowe waves to the fans as Minutemen stand nearby. *Photo courtesy of the* Oregonian.

Clark College. The local college has been in existence since 1867, so the team wasn't going to use that name.

Other names that reached the finalist stage were Trappers, Pride, Ports, Rainbows, RainDrops, Steelheaders, Oregonians, Columbians and Volcanos.

Local resident Eldon Swank was one of the twelve individuals who entered the name Timbers.

"It was one of the first ones I sent in," Swank, who entered an astonishing 152 names, told the *Oregonian* on March 9, 1975. "I sent in five envelopes. No, I didn't buy that many newspapers, but I made prints of the entry form."

Swank also submitted the names of Surf and Pacifics, basing his selections around water.

Seattle held a name-the-team contest in December 1973.

"We feel very strongly that the soccer fans in the area should be heard with regard to naming the team," Walt Daggatt said in a Sounders newsletter. "This, after all, will be their team."

Club officials sifted through three hundred suggestions, and Daggatt announced the six finalist names a month later, on January 13, 1974: Cascades, Evergreens, Mariners, Schooners, Sockeyes and Sounders.

More than 3,700 votes were cast in the final competition, and the Sounders won with 32 percent of the vote. The club had a name, but some people wondered: what's a Sounder?

"We'll have an artist working on that immediately," said Hal Childs, then the club's public relations manager. "One thing for sure, it'll involve a soccer ball."

A note: The "Mariners" name was quickly adopted for Seattle's new Major League Baseball franchise, which began play in 1977.

CREATING THE ROSTERS

Both teams started their existence in roughly the same fashion: signing a bunch of players primarily from England, Scotland, Wales and Northern Ireland. Thirteen of the twenty-one players on the Sounders' initial roster were from either England or Scotland in 1974, while fourteen of the Timbers' initial seventeen roster players hailed from England, Scotland, Wales or Northern Ireland in 1975.

Many of the players had just completed the soccer season in Great Britain, which ran from August through April. The end of the English soccer season left the players with little time for travel to the Pacific Northwest and prepare for the NASL season.

"We had to put a whole new team together, because we didn't have any players," said John Best, the first coach of the Sounders in 1974. "Many of them were playing in leagues (in England), and we were forced to wait until they were through. By the time they got to Seattle, we didn't have a lot of preparation time, about a couple of weeks."

With the clock ticking quickly toward the start of the season, both clubs relied on old connections to England to assemble rosters. Best was born in Liverpool and spent a brief time playing for the storied club and the Tranmere Rovers, a lower-division club in the Liverpool area. Best signed at least four players—defenders Jimmy Gabriel, John Rowlands and Alan Stephens, along with midfielder Roy Sinclair—with ties to the city.

"My background was in England, therefore all my contacts were there. I could easily rely on the reports I received when I tried to make decisions

The 1974 Seattle Sounders team roster. *From 1976 Sounders Yearbook, courtesy of Russ Daggatt.*

John Best was the Sounders' first NASL coach beginning in 1974. *From 1976 Sounders Yearbook, courtesy of Russ Daggatt.*

about players," Best said. "I knew those guys and had seen some of them play in England. They already knew the system I wanted to play, and I figured they could come in and start playing quickly."

Most of the players had never set foot in the United States, let alone in Seattle. The players didn't know it at the time of their arrival, but there was someone within the organization familiar with the British way of life: the managing partner, Walt Daggatt.

"His own parents emigrated to the United States from England and homesteaded in the hills above Lyle, Washington, initially before moving to Portland," Russ Daggatt said. "So he grew up in an English household."

Daggatt immediately connected with the new players.

"It was like he adopted them as his own sons. He came to think of the players as his second family," Russ Daggatt said. "It went beyond the playing field to helping them get their lives together, helping them get jobs outside of soccer. He would help them deal with any personal problems in their lives. He had a real emotional tie to the team."

—— • ——

Vic Crowe, the first coach of the Timbers in 1975, was in the same position as Best prior to their inaugural season. The league awarded an expansion franchise to Portland in January, and the season started in May. The English season didn't end until sometime in late April.

"Most of the players arrived within ten days of the season," Hoban said. "The week before we played Seattle, it was a matter of players introducing themselves to each other."

Crowe was the coach at Aston Villa—then in England's second division—before coming to Portland. Crowe opted to sign a number of players—forward Willie Anderson, midfielders Brian Godfrey and Tony Betts, along with defenders Mick Hoban and Barry Lynch—from the Aston Villa system to the first Timbers squad in 1975. Crowe raided another English team, the Wolverhampton Wanderers. He signed forwards Peter Withe and Chris Dangerfield, along with midfielders Barry Powell and Jimmy Kelly.

"Many of the players played for Aston Villa or many of the clubs within a short radius of one another, and the style of play was relatively similar," Hoban said.

Because he didn't have a lot of time to practice and develop chemistry, Crowe relied on what he knew as a coach in England.

"The system dictated itself, because we only had seventeen players and some of them were Americans," Anderson said. "The system worked really well, because—to be honest—there wasn't much else we could do apart from that because of the limited amount of players and time we had."

The roster, largely assembled with players and coaches from the area surrounding the then working-class city of Birmingham, England, established a reputation as a hardworking and tough group.

"We wanted to show people that we would give 100 percent. The fans knew we were going to play very hard, even if the conditions were tough," Kelly said. "I think the fans realized that we didn't stop playing hard until the game ended."

That blue-collar, lunch-bucket attitude and reputation quickly earned the favor of the fans.

PORTLAND'S 1975 ALL-NASL STARS

Peter Withe

Barry Powell

Graham Day

ALL-NASL TEAMS

POSITION	1st TEAM
Goalkeeper	Peter Bonetti (St. Louis)
Defender	Bob Smith (Philadelphia)
Defender	Mike England (Seattle)
Defender	Werner Roth (New York)
Defender	Farrukh Quraishi (Tampa)
Midfielder	Arfon Griffiths (Seattle)
Midfielder	Ronnie Sharp (Miami)
Midfielder	Antonio Simoes (Boston)
Forward	Steven David (Miami)
Forward	Pele (New York)
Forward	Gordon Hill (Chicago)

POSITION	2nd TEAM	HONORABLE MENTION
Goalkeeper	Ken Cooper (Dallas)	Barry Watling (Seattle)
Defender	Tony Want (Philadelphia)	Tom McConville (Washington)
Defender	Stewart Jump (Tampa)	Dave Gillett (Seattle)
Defender	Ralph Wright (Miami)	Graham Day (Portland)
Defender	Charlie Mitchell (Rochester)	Brian Rowan (Toronto/N.Y.)
Midfielder	Barry Powell (Portland)	Hugh Fisher (Denver)
Midfielder	John Boyle (Tampa)	Wolfgang Suhnholz (Boston)
Midfielder	Bob Hope (Philadelphia)	John Sissons (Tampa)
Forward	Peter Withe (Portland)	Uri Banhoffer (Los Angeles)
Forward	Tommy Ord (Rochester/N.Y.)	Clyde Best (Tampa)
Forward	Stewart Scullion (Tampa)	Derek Smethurst (Tampa)

The Timbers produced a highly successful season in 1975. *Timbers 1976 Season Guide, courtesy of the Portland Timbers.*

Both club's rosters were filled with players who competed in England, and many of the players knew each other very well by the time they arrived in the Pacific Northwest. However, that familiarity quickly turned into heated competition when they reached the stadium and became on-field rivals. Some players were determined to settle scores developed across the pond, while others wanted to establish superiority in this fledgling rivalry and secure bragging rights.

The players may have been unfamiliar with the cities, surroundings and the fans, but they were very familiar with the game. The NASL didn't waste any time developing the Pacific Northwest rivalry between Portland and Seattle.

The Sounders and Timbers would meet in their season opening game in 1975.

"I always thought the Seattle players were a bit cocky," Kelly said. "When we played Seattle…'hatred' may be too strong a word. But we would be thinking, 'Don't let these bastards win this game.'"

Chapter 2
THE GAMES

The games between the two clubs in 1975 featured all the elements that transformed the rivalry into what it is today. Controversial penalty calls. Disputed penalty kicks. Fighting in the stands among supporters. Little did those players and fans know that they were pioneers, starting a long and heated rivalry.

The referee tries to maintain control of a Portland at Seattle game in the North American Soccer League. *Photo courtesy of the Portland Timbers.*

MAY 2, 1975
INAUGURAL GAME AT PORTLAND

The "experienced" Sounders walked into a rain-soaked Civic Stadium, confident of a win.

"We went down there knowing we had already had a year to play together. We thought, 'This is our second year, and they're only in their first year,'" Seattle midfielder/defender Jimmy Gabriel said. "They were just like us in '74, they only had a couple of weeks to be together. They hadn't played a game yet."

They hadn't played a game, but the Timbers knew one thing: they wanted to win their first-ever NASL regular season game, and the result would be particularly sweet coming against the more experienced lads from up north.

With the Timbers dominating play in the game, the Sounders decided the only way to slow down the game was to get physical and foul. The Sounders committed twenty-eight fouls, but it was a foul call against the Timbers that decided the game.

Portland defender Barry Lynch tripped Seattle midfielder Hank Liotart in the penalty box during the 29th minute, a foul the Timbers hotly contested by jumping in the face of the referee.

Gabriel lined up for the penalty kick and calmly placed the ball in the lower right corner—no chance for Portland goalkeeper Graham Brown—for the only score of the game.

Gabriel wasn't the hero for the Sounders: Goalkeeper Barry Watling was the man of the match. The Timbers peppered Watling with twenty-two shots in the game. But Watling was equal to the challenge, stopping the

The Sounders 1975 roster. *Sounders 1976 Yearbook, courtesy of Russ Daggatt.*

Timbers with ten saves, and he saved the game by stoning Portland's Barry Powell's penalty kick in the 48th minute. Even that play was marked with controversy, with Portland claiming Watling came off his line and moved toward the ball too quickly, which would have been a violation.

According to the Timbers' media guide, 8,131 people watched the game, but the *Oregonian* reported the attendance was 6,913. Regardless of the actual number, the fans who did watch witnessed the birth of a rivalry.

———•———

More than 27,000 watched the Timbers win 2–1 in Portland on July 26. A week later, the Sounders won the regular season series with a 3–2 win in overtime in front of a sell-out crowd of 17,925 in Seattle's Memorial Stadium.

The Timbers finished first in the Pacific Division, barely edging…Seattle. Average attendance for NASL games was just below 7,597 a game in 1975, but the Sounders' average attendance of 16,826 a game ranked second in the NASL (only San Jose had more, with 17,927) and the Timbers' average of 14,503 ranked third. The average attendance for three Sounders-Timbers regular season games was 17,788.

League officials, sensing a real opportunity to rake in a few more dollars, pitted the two clubs against each other in a one-game, quarterfinal playoff.

AUGUST 12, 1975
PLAYOFF GAME AT PORTLAND

"Everybody's a bit more keyed up for Seattle. They're raring to go. Even our warm-ups in practice have been a bit more spirited," Portland forward Willie Anderson told the *Oregonian* on August 12, 1975.

Many of the players were still under contract with clubs in England, and with the 1975–76 season already underway, those clubs were demanding they return as soon as possible.

"They told me to come back two weeks early, but I told them, 'I ain't coming back,'" Anderson said. "I said, 'We've got the semifinal and the final. I'm not going to miss that.'"

Portland fans cheer on the Timbers during a game in Seattle on August 2, 1975, at Memorial Stadium. *Photo courtesy of the Portland Timbers.*

The fourth game of the rivalry in 1975 possessed the same characteristics as the first three games: plenty of emotion, physical play, fouls and dominance by the Timbers between the boxes.

"It was a really hard game," Seattle coach John Best said. "Both teams went absolutely flat out."

The players slogged through a heated and physical slugfest (thirty-eight fouls: Portland with fifteen; Seattle, twenty-three). The Timbers took twenty-three shots compared to just three by the Sounders. But the opportunistic Sounders took advantage of one of their three shots to score first in front of 31,523 fans, a record attendance for an NASL playoff game at the time.

Seattle defender John Rowlands scored after an assist from forward Paul Crossley, giving the Sounders the lead early in the second half.

"We felt good about getting that first goal," Gabriel said. "But we also remembered that we had lost after scoring first in the last game we played in Portland." (Portland won 2–1 on July 26.)

The Timbers responded when Portland midfielder Barry Powell was on the end of a cross from Peter Withe and provided the equalizer in the 71st minute, before the game went to sudden-death overtime. A loss for either

The two photos show Tony Betts's game-winning goal as the Timbers defeated the Sounders in overtime in a 1975 playoff game. *Timbers 1976 Season Guide, courtesy of the Portland Timbers.*

team not only meant a quick departure from the playoffs, but it also meant a quick departure from the United States for some players.

"The teams in England wanted us back as soon as possible," Kelly said. "Nobody thought we would have that kind of season as a first-year team. We were supposed to be back on a certain date. We thought as soon as the game was over, the next day, we go back to England."

The players were having too much fun.

"I remember Barry Powell saying to me, 'I don't want to fly back tomorrow. I don't want to go back yet,'" Kelly said.

Forward Tony Betts headed in a cross from Anderson to score the game-winner with 1:29 remaining in the overtime period.

"We wanted this one," Betts told the *Oregonian* on August 14, 1975. "It's bigger than the Super Bowl, or whatever they call it."

Coming off an overtime win (3–2 in Seattle on August 2) against the Timbers in the regular season and watching another lead slip away—especially in their first-ever playoff game—was devastating for the Sounders.

"We felt we should've been able to go down there and match them, and we did for the most part," Gabriel said. "It was terribly disappointing for us and disappointing for our fans. We felt we let Seattle down."

The Sounders weren't the only team in shock. The reaction of the Timbers was one of complete surprise.

"When we scored in sudden-death overtime, it was like a fairy tale," Anderson said.

Fans streamed onto the field, engulfing the players and creating absolute bedlam.

"When you see the reaction of the players and the fans, it was like we won the World Series," Kelly said. "We didn't get off the field for fifteen or twenty minutes."

August 22, 1982
Final NASL Game at Portland

Attendance had plummeted from an all-time rivalry high of 31,523 for the 1975 playoff game down to 9,517 for the game in August 1982. The fan excitement and support generated during that first season in 1975 had dissipated into near indifference seven years later.

"There was talk that the team was looking for a new investor. At that point, there were teams that were beginning to fold in the league," said midfielder John Bain, a member of the Timbers from 1978 to 1982. "We always thought there was going to be a team. We didn't have any indication that was going to be the last season."

Club owner Harry Merlo purchased the Timbers in 1979 and helped the struggling franchise remain afloat. Merlo shelled out plenty of cash to acquire new players such as Robbie Rensenbrink and Willie Donachie, but the infusion of talent didn't spur attendance or help in the win-loss column. The Timbers averaged 8,786 fans a game in 1982, the lowest average in the team's eight years of NASL existence.

Average attendance for NASL games was 13,156 in 1982, but the number was inflated by attendance at New York Cosmos games. The Cosmos averaged 28,749 fans a game that year, more than double the league average. But owners, hemorrhaging money on expensive and aging foreign players, were bailing out of the league.

"Owners talk to owners, and people started freaking out. It was one of those things that when things started to go bad for the league, people who had put money in since 1973–74 no longer wanted to do it," said Bernie Fagan, a member of the Timbers from 1980 to 1982. "Suddenly, the Timbers are in the same situation."

When the Timbers took the field against the Sounders, there was a sense of dread that the end was near. The fans, aware of the Timbers' plight, held up signs during the game that alternately blamed Merlo or the media for the team's seemingly inevitable demise.

The Timbers decided if this was going to be the last game, they were going to go out on top.

"We wanted to win badly for the fans to remember the team," Bain said.

As much as the Timbers wanted to win, the Sounders couldn't afford to lose. They could claim the division title with a win, and they weren't going to let the Timbers' money woes affect their play on the field.

"We had heard about the financial problems in the league, and there were some teams that had already dropped out," Best said. "We didn't know about Portland's situation, but there were some rumors. But we didn't care. We wanted to win the championship."

It was a typical hard-fought game, with both sides missing out on chances.

Bain had two scores nullified because of offside calls, preventing the Timbers from taking a lead. Seattle forward Mark Peterson, who scored 17 goals during the season, scored in the 85th minute.

The Timbers exited the league the same way they entered in 1975, with a 1–0 loss to Seattle.

SEPTEMBER 18, 2005
ELIMINATION AT SEATTLE

The Timbers knew they needed to mark nemesis Roger Levesque after the Seattle forward had burned them with a goal just two minutes into the first game of the two-game, aggregate-goal playoff series in the United Soccer

Leagues (USL) First Division. The Sounders' defense made Levesque's goal stand up to steal a crucial Game 1 win at Portland.

"There's nothing better than beating a rival on their home field. That was always the motivation," Seattle midfielder Leighton O'Brien said. "It's always exciting as a player—even more so to travel and play away from home—because the environment that is created in Portland is fantastic. But beating them in front of their fans, that was always a good feeling."

Levesque, a legitimate scoring threat after scoring seven goals during the regular season in 2005, was just beginning to establish himself in the rivalry after scoring three goals in three games (regular season and playoffs) against the Timbers in 2004.

"We played well, and I had a really good series against them [in 2004]," Levesque said. "They had a good run in the regular season, but we were pretty hot coming in and it was good to beat them."

Knowing he had burned them in Game 1 of the 2005 series, the Timbers' plan was to mark Levesque closely in Game 2.

The Timbers defense wasn't prepared—again—early in the second game. Drawing a bead on a 25-yard free kick from O'Brien, Levesque dove headfirst to redirect the ball past Portland goalkeeper Josh Saunders in the

Seattle forward Roger Levesque (number 18 in white) and defender Zach Scott (number 17 in white) celebrate after scoring a goal against the Timbers. *Photo courtesy of the Portland Timbers.*

fifth minute of play. Levesque's score gave the Sounders a 1–0 lead in the game and a 2–0 lead in aggregate goals in the series.

"We kind of lost track of him again," said Portland defender Scot Thompson, who played in the series. "I feel like he played well and did a good job as opposed to us not doing our homework and not being prepared for him. I really can't take anything away from him."

Levesque wasn't finished torturing the Timbers. Midfielder Andrew Gregor sent a pass inside the box, where the hardworking Levesque had made a run. It was too easy in the 54th minute.

Game—and series—over.

"Roger had a knack for scoring big goals. He scored some amazing goals against Portland," said Brian Schmetzer, Sounders head coach from 2002 to 2008. "He really won the series for us."

The loss was difficult to swallow for the Timbers.

"We had done an unbelievable job of turning our season around just to get into the playoffs," Portland coach Bobby Howe said. "Being knocked out of the playoffs was very disappointing. Especially losing to Seattle again."

The Sounders went on to win the first of two USL First Division championships.

June 26, 2007
Hugo's Revenge at Seattle

One particular player's impact on the game was particularly satisfying for the Sounders and agonizing for the Timbers.

Hugo Alcaraz-Cuellar, a former Portland midfielder, had caused the Sounders plenty of trouble on the field for five seasons. But the Timbers had named Gavin Wilkinson as coach and general manager in April 2007, and Wilkinson decided to clean house by jettisoning twenty-one of the twenty-five players from the 2006 roster.

Alcaraz-Cuellar was one of those players who did not return in 2007. Portland fans were shocked that Alcaraz-Cuellar signed with the Sounders prior to the 2007 season. Alcaraz-Cuellar, who played with the Timbers for five seasons (2002–06), left Portland as the club's all-time leader (USL First Division) in assists and ranked among the club's all-time top ten in games played, minutes, shots and fouls. That kind of longevity and production earned him the status as one of the club's best-known and favorite players.

Justin Thompson's goal after a free kick by Andrew Gregor propelled the Timbers to a 1–0 lead in the 19th minute of the U.S. Open Cup qualifying game. Portland defender Cameron Knowles was red-carded and sent off after throwing an elbow inside the penalty box in the 41st minute.

"It was strange because no one really stepped up to take the kick. We had Sebastien Le Toux who was a forward and scoring goals. I thought he was going to step up and take it, because for me, I like forwards to take PKs because it's a confidence-builder when they score," Alcaraz-Cuellar said. "So I thought he was going to step up and take it because he had been scoring goals really well. Then I thought maybe Roger Levesque would, because he had been with the team for a couple of years.

"I wasn't a guy who would come in and say, 'Let me take the kick.' But no one really stepped up to take it and everyone started looking around. Then someone said, 'Hugo, why don't you take it?' I said, 'Okay, I'll take it.'"

It was a chance for the former Timber to exact some revenge on the club that had kicked him to the curb. Alcaraz-Cuellar buried the penalty kick for the equalizer.

Alcaraz-Cuellar's day was made complete when Seattle defender Jake Besagno scored the game-winning goal in the 70th minute, giving the Sounders a 2–1 win and bouncing the Timbers out of the Open Cup competition.

"It was no big deal. Just a penalty kick. We were down 1–0, it was obviously very important to score," Alcaraz-Cuellar said. "I had a responsibility to [Seattle general manager] Adrian [Hanauer] and [Seattle head coach] Brian [Schmetzer], the Seattle fans and my teammates to play like a Seattle Sounder. I think that kick made them realize that I was committed to Seattle."

August 7, 2008
Final USL Game at Portland

Knowing the Sounders were on their way up to the big time of MLS the following year and about to leave them behind, the rejected and irritated Timbers approached the game with a surly attitude.

"The whole team had that chip on their shoulder," said Scot Thompson, a Portland defender from 2004 to 2010. "Anytime you get to play against Seattle, who was about to make the jump, any player will tell that you're always trying to prove to that coach that cut you or to that fan that says you're not good enough that you're better."

With the players knowing that the game could be the last in the rivalry for a long time, possibly forever, the pressure was intense by game time.

"Every time we stepped on the pitch against Portland, it was always going to be heated. Just a battle," said Josh Gardner, a midfielder with Seattle in 2007 and 2008. "We knew this game would be even more heated since we were going to MLS and they weren't."

Le Toux scored the only goal in the game—he tapped in a ball from five yards out after the ball had deflected to him, the result of a shot by Nik Besagno that hit the post—in the 20th minute, giving the Sounders a 1–0 win.

By the time referee Jasen Anno blew the final whistle, he had issued six yellow cards, one red card and called twenty-four fouls (twelve for Seattle, twelve for Portland).

The chippiness began when Gardner was given a yellow card for a late tackle on Portland midfielder Bryan Jordan in the 15th minute. The chippiness turned into nastiness after Portland defender Cameron Knowles received a yellow card for throwing an elbow into Le Toux's jaw while the two were fighting for the ball in the 31st minute.

The game turned ugly two minutes later, when Thompson came in late and cut down Gardner—the two are friends but have their own personal

Longtime friends off the field, Seattle midfielder Josh Gardner (left) and Portland defender Scot Thompson were fierce enemies on the field. *Photo courtesy of the Portland Timbers.*

on-field rivalry—after he had played the ball away, prompting Anno to give Thompson a questionable straight red card.

"It was a late tackle, but a tackle I've done thousands of times. I wasn't coming in to be dirty, I was coming in to try and tackle him and the ball," Thompson said. "He got a toe poke around me, just as I was coming in to tackle. I came in a second late and got him."

Seattle coach Brian Schmetzer said Thompson's tackle didn't warrant the defender being sent off.

"I remember Thompson not getting the best call in that game," Schmetzer said. "We thought the red card was a little harsh."

The Sounders ended their rivalry against the Timbers in the USL First Division era the same way they started and ended their NASL rivalry against the Timbers with a 1–0 win.

July 1, 2009
48 Seconds at Portland

A sight previously unseen for a soccer game in Portland…

"I need tickets!" said the man, waving tickets in his hand while walking up and down the block of S.W. Morrison adjacent to PGE Park. Anybody got tickets?"

Ticket scalpers roaming the streets, in search of buyers and sellers? Normally, those guys are patrolling the Rose Garden area, negotiating deals for Portland Trail Blazer tickets, not Portland Timbers tickets.

The buzz descending on PGE Park was palpable on a warm and sunny evening. Two hours before the game, Portland and Seattle fans were already milling around the stadium. Some Seattle fans had arrived by bus while others made the three-hour drive south on Interstate 5.

Inside the stadium, the electricity was growing as kick-off grew closer with a Portland modern-franchise-record 16,382 fans packing PGE Park. The electricity had also oozed its way inside each team's locker room.

"I didn't need to get the team fired up. All they had to do was walk by the fans outside on their way to the locker room or see the fans in the stadium during warm-ups," said Gavin Wilkinson, the Timbers' head coach in 2009. "They knew the game was special."

The Timbers had lost just one of their first fifteen games (9–1–5) in all competitions and were unbeaten in twelve consecutive games of USL First

Division play. (The Timbers went on to set a USL First Division record of twenty-four consecutive games without a loss that season.)

The Sounders were in the middle of their inaugural season in Major League Soccer. Seattle had taken MLS by storm, setting attendance records in nearly every home game, and the Sounders had posted a record of 6–3–7 in MLS regular season play and an 8–3–7 record in all competitions leading up to the Open Cup game against the Timbers. The numbers were impressive for an expansion club.

"No way were we going to lose to them," Levesque said. "Nobody wanted to play more than myself, Sebastien [Le Toux] and Zach Scott. The guys that made the transition from the USL club to the MLS Sounders."

For the Timbers, the Open Cup game against the Sounders was their World Cup final. A win against an MLS team would be a major victory for a team that's aspiring to reach MLS. They planned to come out with an energy that would catch the Sounders by surprise.

"We saw this as a game where we could show where we were at as a team," Wilkinson said. "And we wanted to make the point that while they may be able to beat us in football, we could beat them in effort and working a little bit harder. I told them to make sure they put on a great performance."

The crowd was on the edge of their seats by the time the players came out for warm-ups.

"It was electrifying and nerve-wracking," Wilkinson said. "I've played in front of some big crowds. But as far as coaching in Portland and being involved as general manager in Portland, the atmosphere was simply electrifying. I still get goose bumps thinking about it and remembering what it was like."

Flares were being lit in the stands, smoke bombs were ignited and the fans were screaming in anticipation as the players walked out onto the field.

"Just…an…incredible atmosphere," said Seattle defender Taylor Graham, who did not play because of a broken bone in his foot. "Absolutely amazing."

The Timber fans' smiles turned to frowns before they were comfortably seated as their nemesis, Roger Levesque, caught the Timbers by surprise and drove a stake into the their hearts once again.

Levesque, flying parallel to the turf, got his head on a cross from Sanna Nyassi, sending the ball flying past Portland goalkeeper Steve Cronin and into the back of the net just 48 seconds into the game.

"Everyone was kind of in shock, to be honest," Levesque said. "I mean, it's only a minute into the game."

The loud atmosphere created by the fans fostered an environment that helped lead to Levesque's stunner.

Sounders versus Timbers

Seattle forward Roger Levesque (number 24) heads the ball in front of Portland defender Scot Thompson during the Seattle at Portland U.S. Open Cup game at PGE Park on July 1, 2009. *Photo courtesy of the Portland Timbers.*

Sounders supporters celebrate the goal scored by Roger Levesque during the Seattle at Portland U.S. Open Cup game at PGE Park on July 1, 2009. *Photo courtesy of the Portland Timbers.*

"I remember it was so loud, and there was so much energy," Portland defender Scot Thompson said. "I was yelling at [center back] Cam [Cameron Knowles] that Roger was coming across the middle. Cam couldn't hear me at all, and Roger was able to squeeze in there and get that goal."

Stephen King scored in the 27th minute to give the Sounders a 2–0 lead. Mandjou Keita got one back for the Timbers in the second half, but that wasn't enough, and the Sounders won 2–1. However, all anyone remembers is 48 seconds.

May 14, 2011
New Beginnings at Seattle

The driving rain didn't dampen the enthusiasm and excitement surrounding the first-ever MLS regular season game in the rivalry.

"I think the amount of energy and enthusiasm that the Portland fans have brought to an already existing rivalry, to a team that has done it first— meaning our fans, our crowd, our record, our Open Cup, our victories—it adds to it," Seattle assistant coach Brian Schmetzer told the *Seattle Times* on May 10, 2011. "It gives us something to make sure we're not complacent and we're continuing to try and push up and onward because there are guys nipping at our heels."

The rivalry, relentlessly hyped by MLS throughout the week, was broadcast on national television by ESPN2 and ESPN Deportes. The broadcast reportedly reached a potential audience in 116 countries and 40 million households outside the United States. Seattle and Portland fans from as far away as South Korea, the Ukraine and South America organized viewing parties to watch the game.

The Portland fans, chanting loudly, arrived in Seattle by the busloads and entered the stadium through a special gate—European style—far away from the Seattle fans.

The constant and heavy rain falling throughout the game resulted in sloppy play, with neither club able to take control in front of 36,593 fans. The uneven play didn't affect the intensity of the game, which took on a physical nature. The Sounders didn't want to give the upstart expansion club any reason to believe they were on the same level.

"You want to beat the big brother. We've done well since we've been in MLS, and the Timbers always want to beat the brother that's done well,"

Seattle midfielder Servando Carrasco (left) and Portland center back Eric Brunner challenge for a header during the Portland at Seattle game on May 14, 2011, at CenturyLink Field. *Photo courtesy of the Seattle Sounders.*

Schmetzer said. "You want to show that you're as good—or better—as your big brother."

The Sounders sent their fans into a frenzy when midfielder Alvaro Fernandez gathered in a pretty flick from Fredy Montero and drilled a left-footed volley inside the near post and past Portland goalkeeper Troy Perkins in the 52nd minute.

Portland defender Mamadou "Futty" Danso celebrates after scoring a goal during the Portland at Seattle game at Qwest Field on May 14, 2011. *Photo courtesy of the Portland Timbers.*

"When I saw the play shaping up I started yelling and calling [for the ball], especially when I saw the two defenders going after Fredy," Fernandez told reporters after the game. "After the flick I was one on one in front of the goalkeeper, and I was able to finalize."

The Timbers, who had established a reputation of being dangerously effective on set pieces, burned the Sounders on a free kick. Jack Jewsbury's kick from 45 yards away sent the ball into the box where six-foot-three defender Mamadou "Futty" Danso was waiting. Danso rose above the Seattle defense, beat Sounders goalkeeper Kasey Keller to the ball and headed the ball into the back of the net for the equalizing goal in the 65th minute.

"It was something that we had been practicing throughout [the] week. We just want Jack to hit the ball out in front. Just like David Beckham," Danso said after the game. "If we could hit the ball in front of Kasey Keller, it's going to be like a fifty-fifty. The ball got on my head, and I just had to put it on target."

June 24, 2012
Seeing Red at Portland

Lovel Palmer made his decision in an instant and in the heat of the moment. He ran up from behind and delivered a forearm to the back of the head of Seattle forward Eddie Johnson.

"I saw Johnson, he went at Futty," Palmer said. "I'm thinking, 'Naw. There's no way I'm gonna let someone—especially in a rivalry game—go at my teammate like that.' I just reacted."

Palmer's WWF-esque move earned him a straight red card and an automatic ejection that highlighted a near-mêlée in the waning moments of the Timbers' 2–1 win at Jeld-Wen Field.

Palmer's dismissal occurred one minute after Seattle forward Fredy Montero was told to take an early shower after the last of a series of snotty incidents that ignited the ruckus in stoppage time. The dueling red cards culminated a fierce game in which the heated emotions, physical play and trash-talking pushed the rivalry to a new level of intensity.

Portland midfielder Darlington Nagbe breaks up a confrontation between Portland forward Kris Boyd and Seattle forward Fredy Montero (far right), while an assistant referee tries to separate Seattle forward Eddie Johnson (number 7) and Portland defender David Horst (left) during the Seattle at Portland game at Jeld-Wen Field on June 24, 2012. *Photo courtesy of the Portland Timbers.*

Seattle defender Patrick Ianni (right) looks ready for a battle while being restrained by Portland defender Mamadou "Futty" Danso during the Seattle at Portland game at Jeld-Wen Field on June 24, 2012. *Photo courtesy of the Portland Timbers.*

"Every time we play them, whether it's preseason, Open Cup, whatever, there's always bad blood and it's always a nasty game," Seattle midfielder Brad Evans said.

Evans made the statement BEFORE the game. Little did he realize that his assessment of the rivalry would prove to be very accurate.

⎯⎯•⎯⎯

What any rivalry needs is some bulletin-board material from a player saying something that is sure to irk the rival and increase the tension. Evans was happy to fan the flames of the rivalry by dissing the Timbers' club and its fans. He was the instigator of a more personal and pointed round of trash-talking that commenced days before kickoff.

Responding to a question about the competitiveness of the rivalry, Evans said the Sounders organization was, frankly, better than the Timbers, regardless of which team won the game.

"You can definitely, obviously tell that our organization is just a cut above," Evans said. "If I talk to those guys, they'll say the same thing. It is what it is. And that's going to fuel the fire."

Evans wasn't finished disrespecting the Timbers. He called out the Timbers fans—particularly the Timbers Army—labeling them as a bunch of drunks.

"It's a bunch of drunk, mid-thirties type of crowd who are very well educated," Evans said. "Much more vocal. A little bit more crazy. It's a little nastier playing down there."

Evans's statement contains more than a nugget of truth, but for someone from the Sounders to call out the opposition fans on the eve of the big game bordered on blasphemous, and the Timbers fans responded with vitriol.

"Evans is a dolt: has he looked at the Sounders fans that travel to Portland? I had a good view of them: mostly obese or at least very overweight, drunk, beer slinging males and females. Some had obscene gestures for families and young girls nearby. Disgusting!" said one fan in *Oregon Live* on June 22, 2012. In the June 22, 2012 edition of the *Seattle Times*, a Seattle fan fired back, "Let's see I think I called them 'Portscum,' compared them to a port-a-potty, called the team amateur (since they couldn't even beat one), and failed at log cutting." The insults were flying up and down Interstate 5. And the game was still two days away.

* • *

Portland fans groaned with collective pain and Seattle supporters held their breath after a header by an unmarked David Horst sent the ball toward the net for what looked like a sure goal, but the ball hit the crossbar and bounced away in the 11th minute.

The Timbers drew first blood when Scottish striker Kris Boyd slipped past center back Jhon Kennedy Hurtado—the Sounders wanted an offside call—and easily scored by slotting in a crossing pass from fellow Scotsman Steven Smith in the 16th minute of the game.

The crossbar had prevented Horst from scoring earlier in the game, but he wouldn't be denied on a second chance. Once again, the Sounders didn't mark Horst closely enough, and he raced inside the box and—while being pushed by Seattle defender Jeff Parke—found himself on the end of Portland midfielder Franck Songo'o's perfectly placed corner kick.

Portland defender David Horst celebrates scoring a goal as Seattle defender Jeff Parke reacts during the Seattle at Portland game at Jeld-Wen Field on June 24, 2012. *Photo courtesy of the Portland Timbers.*

Timbers Army fans chant and cheer during a game at Jeld-Wen Field. *Photo courtesy of the Portland Timbers.*

After watching his first header send the ball directly into the crossbar, Horst angled his head to punch the ball downward. The ball bounced to the left of diving goalkeeper Andrew Webber and to the right of midfielder Alex Caskey, who whiffed on his attempt to head the ball out before falling over on top of Webber.

"I got the taste in the first header that hit the crossbar, and Franck put the ball in the exact same spot again," Horst said. "I headed it down this time, instead of up. It worked out the second time. It felt pretty good, especially in this rivalry."

The green smoke rose skyward in front of the Timbers Army section inside Jeld-Wen Field, signaling a goal scored by the home club, and the Sounders were wondering how they had allowed Horst yet another uncontested header inside the box.

"We missed our mark completely [on the first goal]. [On the second] the guy wins a free header in the box," Weber told the *Tacoma News Tribune*. "I thought I was going to save it, and me and Caskey collided."

The delirious crowd roared "PT! FC! PT! FC!" as the Timbers walked off the field, carrying a 2–0 lead at halftime.

The Sounders, who hadn't lost to the Timbers in two MLS regular season games in 2011 and carried an air of superiority—at least according to Evans—in the rivalry, didn't want to see that streak end in the first game of the series in 2012. The Sounders came out firing in the second half. From shots on goal and fouls to simply outworking the Timbers, the Sounders asserted themselves and forced the Timbers to recoil.

The aggressiveness paid off in the 58th minute when Eddie Johnson fought off a gambling Horst for a fifty-fifty ball. The Seattle striker raced into the upper left corner of the box, eluded Horst once again and cut back to his left to lose Mamadou "Futty" Danso and create space. Johnson then wound up a beautiful left-footed shot that sent the ball sailing past a diving Troy Perkins into the upper left corner of the net.

The Sounders fans, dormant for much of the game, leapt to their feet and as if on cue, transformed into a flag-waving, towel-twirling throng. Johnson's score sliced the Timbers lead in half, 2–1. "We just had to wake up," Johnson said.

With 32 minutes remaining in the second half, it was game on. Knowing the mentally fragile Timbers have been known to concede a second—even third—goal after allowing the initial goal in games during the season, the energized Sounders continued to press their attack, hoping to break down the Timbers.

Seattle fans erupt with joy and, perhaps just as important, hope and energy after Sounders forward Eddie Johnson scores a goal to cut the Timbers lead to 2–1 in the 58th minute during the game at Portland's Jeld-Wen Field on June 24, 2012. *Anatoliy Lukich.*

Tension begins to rise during the second half of the Seattle at Portland game at Jeld-Wen Field on June 24, 2012. *Photo courtesy of the Portland Timbers.*

While most of the Sounders were trying to produce the equalizing goal through their play on the field, Seattle forward Fredy Montero tried a different tactic: Rattle the Timbers mentally. Not letting his small (five-foot-nine, 172 pounds) stature deter him, Montero, who had already shoved Franck Songo'o in the third minute of play, ramped up his efforts to start a confrontation with anyone wearing a Timbers jersey.

Montero was called for a foul after using a scissor kick to chop down Portland forward Darlington Nagbe and then argued with the referee in the 51st minute. Montero was called for another foul after taking down Nagbe a second time in the 56th minute. Nursing a 2–1 lead midway through the second half and the referee awarding Seattle a throw-in, Portland midfielder Jack Jewsbury used his foot to nudge the ball down the field a few yards in an obvious move to kill time. An incensed Montero ran up to Jewsbury, confronted him chest-to-chest and then pushed Jewsbury aside.

Montero saw the second half of Johnson and Horst exchanging shoves—Johnson first, Horst retaliating—near the top of the Portland box. Protecting his teammate, Montero rushed over and, using two hands, pushed Horst.

Seattle forward Eddie Johnson (lower) gets the worst of the exchange between Portland defender David Horst (above Johnson) and Seattle defender Andy Rose (right) during the Seattle at Portland game at Jeld-Wen Field on June 24, 2012. *Photo courtesy of the Portland Timbers.*

The Portland center back, beginning his post-soccer acting career and immediately thrusting himself into contention for the best actor award, fell as if he had been hit by a stray bullet in a gang drive-by shooting.

"This guy was head-to-head with Eddie, and I just tried to push him away," Montero said after the game. "He fell to the ground."

Referee Ricardo Salazar yanked out his red card, and Montero's day came to an abrupt end.

"Today wasn't that great of a day for me," Montero told the *Seattle Times* on June 25, 2012. "Things went wrong towards the end and they got out of control to the point where I had to leave."

Johnson and Danso started exchanging shoves, nearly coming to fisticuffs before being separated. Palmer joined the party, with his forearm arriving first.

"We won the game, so at the end of the day, it was worth it," Palmer said. "He was going at my teammate, and I had to let Futty know that I had his back.

"I have no regrets."

October 7, 2012
Making History at Seattle

Sigi Schmid said the feeling was like being in heaven on Earth. In front of a massive home crowd and a national television audience, with his enlarged face draped on a massive pre-game tifo and in need of a late-season win, his Sounders produced a near-perfect performance and dominated the Timbers. Could it get any better for a coach who has won just about every soccer honor possible in the United States? He didn't think so.

"When I walked on the field, I said to [assistant coach Brian Schmetzer], 'This is what heaven must be like,'" Schmid said. "In my imagination of heaven, this is it—packed house, beat Portland by three, fans going crazy, it can't get better than that."

———•———

The Timbers were making their only visit to Seattle during the 2012 season, creating a striking environment of energy and excitement inside CenturyLink Field.

The Timbers needed a win or a draw to clinch the Cascadia Cup, a fan-created competition between the three Northwest teams (Seattle, Portland, Vancouver) in MLS. Finishing off a disastrous season, the Timbers viewed winning the Cascadia Cup as salvaging a small source of pride.

"It's a chance to get something out of this season. Anytime you have a chance to beat the Seattle Sounders and take the cup away from them and give it to our fans, that's a great opportunity," Portland forward Bright Dike said. "We haven't had the best season; it would be something positive to take toward next season."

The Sounders needed to win, not only to keep the Cascadia Cup in Seattle, but they were also locked in a tight race for playoff positioning in the Western Conference. Seattle had already clinched a playoff berth, but the Sounders were aiming for second or third place in the conference to avoid having to play an unpredictable, one-game, single-elimination playoff game.

"The Cascadia Cup is a plus and something that our fans obviously want to retain and something that we want to retain," midfielder Brad Evans said. "But at the end of the day, we want to give ourselves the best chance in the playoffs that we can."

The Emerald City Supporters are ready for the Portland at Seattle game at CenturyLink Field on October 7, 2012. *Geoffrey C. Arnold.*

With so much on the line, few were surprised when the Sounders announced that more than 66,000 tickets had been sold two days before the game. The announced crowd was 66,452 at kickoff, the second-largest stand-alone (non-double-header game) attendance in league history.

"I knew this would be a historic event as it was leading into this weekend," said MLS commissioner Don Garber, who attended the game.

If the game was heaven on earth for Schmid, it was just the opposite—hell on earth—for the Timbers.

Seattle center midfielder Osvaldo Alonso sent a pretty through ball that midfielder Christian Tiffert allowed to go through to right back Adam Johansson, who gathered the ball at full speed during the 25th minute. By the time Portland center back David Horst had marked Johansson, Johansson was already inside the box and rifled a crossing pass to forward Fredy Montero, who was taking dead aim at the net just outside the 6-yard box.

Portland center back Mamadou "Futty" Danso, a step behind Montero, was forced to extend his leg in an attempt to stop the cross. He stopped the cross, but the ball deflected off his foot and into the net for an own goal.

Sensing the Timbers were vulnerable, the Sounders stepped up their attack. With the Sounders pressing deep into Timbers' territory, Evans whipped in a cross to a wide-open Eddie Johnson, who wheeled around and smashed a half-volley shot that zipped past Portland goalkeeper Donovan Ricketts 3 minutes after Danso's own goal. The Sounders led 2–0, and though there were 62 minutes left to be played, this one was over (Montero scored in the 62nd minute to make the final score 3–0).

The embarrassing loss meant the Timbers, who could've clinched the Cascadia Cup with a win or a draw, blew another chance in Seattle. They squandered their first opportunity to clinch the cup with a 1–1 draw against the Sounders—the Timbers needed to win—in Portland on September 15.

"We just didn't show up," Horst said.

Note: The two teams have played 79 games in the series at the close of the 2012 MLS regular season. The team records are: Seattle, 41 wins; Portland, 28 wins; 10 draws.

Chapter 3
THE PLAYERS

ROGER LEVESQUE

He's been called the "Timbers Killer" and has driven a dagger into the hearts of Rose City soccer fans on numerous occasions by scoring critical goals to help the Sounders defeat the Timbers. Then he rubs it in the faces of the Portland fans with a creative—Portland fans would say obnoxious—celebration.

The former Stanford star wasn't the most athletic or flashy player, but his work ethic and nose for the ball means his goals didn't come by accident. Many of his goals against Portland in First Division and U.S. Open Cup play have been, well, killers.

"Roger has scored some important goals against the Timbers," said Brian Schmetzer, Sounders head coach from 2002 to 2008. "So I think that just added to Portland's feelings about him and why they don't like him."

Levesque scored all three of the Sounders' goals in their two-game, aggregate-goal series win (3–0) that eliminated Portland in the USL First Division first-round playoff series in 2005, the year the Sounders won the First Division championship.

Levesque, who joined the Sounders in 2003 before retiring in July 2012, scored his most famous goal of the rivalry against the Timbers in a third-round game of the 2009 U.S. Open Cup. The Open Cup contest was the first game between the two clubs since the Sounders had joined MLS. The First Division Timbers wanted to prove to the Sounders they were as good as the MLS Sounders.

Seattle forward Roger Levesque (in white) and Portland defender Garrett Marcum battle for the ball during a Seattle at Portland game. *Photo courtesy of the Portland Timbers.*

Much to the Timbers Army's chagrin, Levesque—as has been his habit in the rivalry—immediately surfaced. Just 48 seconds into the game and before a Portland First Division record crowd of 16,382 had settled in for the game, the forward laid out for a cross by Sanna Nyassi and his header found the back of the net.

Forty-eight seconds.

"That goal was huge and helped us a ton. Quieting a crowd like that, it was a great feeling for the team," Levesque said. "The biggest thing is the confidence it provides, and you're thinking, 'Okay, now they have to come at us.'"

The Timbers fans were quiet and probably silently grumbling about yet another goal by the hated Levesque. And if the goal wasn't enough, Levesque unveiled a classic celebratory skit just for the Portland fans after engaging in a hug with teammate Sebastien Le Toux.

Levesque ran to a spot near the middle of the field, with teammate Nate Jaqua sprinting behind. He suddenly stopped, stood ramrod straight, as Jaqua, impersonating a lumberjack and wielding an imaginary axe, pretended to "cut down" the tree. Levesque fell backward—mimicking a fallen tree ("Tiiiiiiimber!!")—and crashed to the turf.

"The celebration that took place between Nate [Jaqua] and Roger with the chopping of the tree in the U.S. Open Cup was classic," Seattle defender Taylor Graham said. "Roger was very creative with those celebrations, and he really enjoyed doing something to get under the skin of the Timbers Army."

CLIVE CHARLES

The gargantuan tifo, horizontally blanketing five full sections of the stadium and stretching vertically from the turf to the rafters of Jeld-Wen Field, was raised.

And there was his face, complete with the familiar Afro, plastered in the middle of the banner before the Timbers' game against Seattle on June 24, 2012. He is the only Portland player to have his number retired, and he is among three players in the franchise's "Ring of Honor," inside Jeld-Wen Field.

The face is very familiar to Clyde Best, recalling that he and Charles were teammates on West Ham's youth team in England during the early 1970s.

"Clive's mom put me up when I first went to England. We lived together," Best said. "He was a like a brother."

The bond continued when the two were teammates in Portland.

"I was the one that got Clive to come to Portland. I was playing in Holland at the time. Clive gave me a call and said he wanted to come to North America. I called Don Megson and Don Megson signed him," Best said. "We were always together. We were across the street from one another when we first moved to Portland."

Defender Clive Charles played for the NASL Timbers from 1978 to 1981. *Photo courtesy of the Portland Timbers.*

Charles, a defender from London, wore a Timbers jersey for four seasons (1978–81) but really produced two solid seasons when he played in 54 games during his first two seasons. An injury-plagued Charles appeared in just 13 games in his final two seasons with Portland.

"Clive was a funny guy, he always had something funny to say. He could keep the dressing room bubbly," Best said.

Charles retired from professional soccer and took a job as soccer coach at Reynolds High School in Troutdale, Oregon, in 1983. That's when his coaching career started to eclipse his playing career.

Acting on a tip from former Portland teammate Bernie Fagan, he took the job as head coach of the University of Portland men's soccer team in 1986 and was named coach of the Pilots' women's team in 1989.

"He had amazing talents that were over and above just being a soccer player and a soccer coach," Fagan said. "I just knew all he needed was an opportunity. He knew how to grasp [talented] players and develop them."

Charles slowly built the Pilots—particularly the women's team—into a national power.

The Portland Pilots won the NCAA women's soccer championship in 2002, and Charles guided the early careers of superstars Tiffeny Milbrett, Shannon McMillan and Christine Sinclair. He also molded the careers of Kasey Keller, Steve Cherundolo, Conor Casey and Nate Jaqua.

Preston Burpo

His mug appeared on a banner so large that it consumed an entire lower section at CenturyLink Field as the Sounders fans roared their approval. The image was part of the "Decades of Dominance" tifo unveiled by Seattle supporters before the Seattle-Portland game in May 2011.

"I had to say it blew me away. It was pretty cool," Burpo said. "To kind of get thrown into the Sounders legend mix, it was pretty humbling."

Burpo's longevity and championship pedigree in Seattle established him as one of the greatest goalkeepers in Seattle history and elevated him to near idol-like status among the supporters. Burpo spent nine years with the First Division and A-League Sounders, notching 38 shutouts in 143 appearances. He helped Seattle win the USL First Division championship in 2005, and he was selected as the most valuable player of the Sounders' win against Richmond in the title game.

"We slipped into the playoffs that year," Burpo said. "Then we went on one of those runs—we played pretty well, and we got a couple of lucky bounces."

After Seattle defeated Portland in the first round, the Sounders defeated Montreal in a two-game, aggregate-goal series before more fortuitous bounces in the penalty kick stage of the game helped Seattle win the championship at Qwest Field. The Sounders took a 2–0 lead in PKs but missed their next two while Richmond converted to tie at 2–2. The Kickers missed a chance to win the game in the fifth round before Scott Jenkins—playing in his final professional game before retiring—converted to win the title.

"It was a combination of a team that played well in the playoffs getting a couple of lucky bounces, and we ended up getting a trophy that year," Burpo said. "It sure was a fun year, and that capped off my Seattle Sounders time."

Burpo signed his first MLS contract with Chivas USA in the spring of 2006 after his strong showing in 2005. He then bounced around between Chivas, San Jose and Colorado—a combined total of 46 appearances during that span—before a fateful trade that sent him and Cory Gibbs to New England for Wells Thompson and Jeff Larentowicz in January 2010.

With starter Matt Reis still recovering from offseason shoulder and knee surgery, Burpo was in the Revolution's starting 11 to open the 2010 season. Burpo and the Revolution were struggling with a 2–6–2 record going into their home game against the New York Red Bulls, a game that included a horrific injury that ended Burpo's career.

CLYDE BEST

Coming off his first season with the Timbers, the "Big Man" signed a "lovely" one-year contract to stay with the Timbers.

"Just put it this way: I'm very satisfied with what I got," Best told the *Oregonian* on February 13, 1978. "Everything has worked out quite lovely."

The six-foot-two, 190-pound striker responded to the new contract by scoring a club-high 12 goals and added 9 assists while leading the Timbers to the NASL conference finals in 1978. Even though the Timbers were defeated by New York, Best scored 2 goals during the playoff run.

Best was a valued commodity in the league, and the Timbers were competing with other teams—including Seattle—for the striker's services after the 1978 season. The two parties signed a one-year deal worth more than $30,000 after weeks of protracted negotiations.

Best responded with 8 goals and 8 assists in 1979 and 11 goals and 6 assists in 1980. But Vic Crowe returned as head coach (he coached the team in 1975 and 1976) midway through the 1980 season, marking the fourth coach (Brian Tiler, Don Megson, Peter Warner) in Best's four seasons with the club. The relationship between the easygoing Best and the hard-nosed Crowe seemed fine during the season, but the partnership quickly soured.

"Vic told me what he expected from me and the type player he knew I could be," Best said. "Then we came to the indoor season after my operation and I'm left on the outside."

Best played in just 6 of 18 games during the indoor season after having intestinal surgery.

Forward Clyde Best played for the NASL Timbers for five seasons (1977–81). His 38 goals rank second on the club's all-time list. *Photo courtesy of the Portland Timbers.*

"I didn't take too kindly to that. Don't tell me one thing and do something else," Best said. "That's when everything went downhill."

Teammate John Bain said Best wasn't happy with not playing.

"When you're not playing as much as you think you should be, you're always teed off at the manager," Bain said. "You think you're not getting a fair shake."

Best thought Crowe wasn't interested in playing him, particularly after the arrival of forward Ally Brown (on loan from West Bromwich Albion) and midfielder Barry Powell (on loan from Derby County). Best sensed as much when the 1981 outdoor season started, and he reacted with a disinterested attitude during training and games.

"I felt that if I couldn't make the sixteen- or seventeen-player game roster, it didn't make sense for me being there," Best said. "I didn't like that sort of treatment. I went in and told Vic I wanted to be traded."

Best played in just four games for the Timbers in 1981 before he was traded to Toronto.

"I just didn't like what was going on, never knowing if I was playing or not," Best said. "It wasn't so much that I had no incentive to play. It was just that I didn't like the guessing. I wanted to know where I stood."

Best may or may not have known where he stood under Crowe, but he certainly let Crowe know where the coach stood after he arrived in Toronto.

"As for Vic and Paddy [assistant coach Pat McMahon], well, I just don't give a damn about them," Best told the *Oregonian* on June 21, 1981.

Jimmy Gabriel

The Timbers quickly learned that you didn't mess with Jimmy Gabriel. The Sounders outside back from Dundee, Scotland, wasted little time establishing himself as a physical force during the Seattle-Portland game on July 26, 1975.

"I was never scared of anybody," Gabriel said.

Battling for a fifty-fifty ball, Gabriel grabbed Portland defender Brian Godfrey and threw him to the turf in the 9th minute of the game. Referee Gordon Hill told the Seattle defender to cut out the rough play.

Gabriel ignored Hill's order.

Gabriel delivered an elbow to the mouth of Portland defender Ray Martin—a tough guy in his own right. Blood gushing from his mouth,

Seattle midfielder/defender Jimmy Gabriel (middle, white jersey) was the team's captain before going on to become the head coach in 1977. *Photo courtesy of Seattle Sounders.*

Martin crumbled to the turf and remained down for a few minutes before continuing to play. Not yet finished with his physical tactics, Gabriel slammed into Godfrey with yet another shove in the back.

Portland coach Vic Crowe wasn't surprised and expected that type of play from Gabriel in a rivalry game. Even if Gabriel was thirty-five years old at the time.

"He caused a lot of problems," Crowe told the *Oregonian* on July 27, 1975. "He's an old veteran whose legs don't carry him as far as they used to, but he still causes a lot of problems."

An unapologetic Gabriel said that was just the way he played and part of the game.

"I would jump up, get knocked down. I always did that. Sometimes, people would get hurt in the air. Sometimes, I got hurt," Gabriel said. "I went over the top a wee bit more that I should've done. It was my job to tackle and if I got hurt, well, too bad. If they got hurt, too bad for them. But I was gonna try and win that ball."

GRAHAM DAY

If a foul was called, an altercation surfaced or a yellow or red card was issued, it's likely Day was involved or wasn't too far from the scene. The big (six-foot-one, 170 pounds) center back was another one of those hard-nosed, blue-collar, "I am not going to take any ----" type of players that had come to define the Timbers during their NASL era under coaches Vic Crowe and Don Megson. He set all-time, single-season team records with two ejections in 1975 and six cautions in 1978.

"He had a never-say-die attitude, and he gave you everything that he had," forward Clyde Best said. "He trained hard, and he played hard. And he didn't back down from anybody."

Day's willingness to play physical was on display during the Timbers' 2–1 loss at San Jose on June 14. Day and San Jose defender Derek Craig started wrestling before tempers flared and the two traded punches. Both players were given straight red cards and ejected from the game in the 55th minute.

An all-out mêlée between players, coaches and fans ensued.

Day's on-field tough-guy image was a stark contrast to his very irreverent personality away from the game. He was a cigarette-smoking jokester in the locker room around friends and teammates.

"We used to call him 'Sharky,'" Best said. "He was such a funny character. He always made you laugh—him and Clive Charles."

One of the lasting memories of Day is his now famous—or is it infamous?—prank involving Portland city councilwoman Mildred Schwab. Schwab was standing nearby during player introductions before a game. When Day's name was called, instead of sprinting out onto the field, Day grabbed Schwab, gently laid her down on a nearby medical stretcher and planted a kiss on her. Just as quickly, he picked up the startled Schwab and then ran onto the field.

"He was the clown in the dressing room," Bain said. "He just got all the guys going, and Clive Charles was a hilarious guy as well. Clive and Graham would just have everybody in stitches when we used to travel."

Day even joked about his "rugged" good looks.

"He had this book that had some lists that included the five ugliest players in the league. Graham was voted number two," Bain said. "He was always joking that he wasn't as ugly as people thought."

SEBASTIEN LE TOUX

The Frenchman by way of Dallas had no idea about the rivalry when he signed with the First Division Sounders in 2007.

"I didn't even know about it, because I'm from France," Le Toux said. "I didn't know it was a big rivalry."

He would be brought up to speed quickly. His first game in a Seattle uniform was against…Portland.

"I heard about it, especially from the fans. They would come and say, 'You know, you have to beat Portland.' I would ask, 'Why?' They would say, 'You have to beat Portland, because if we lose, we can't go in Portland,'" Le Toux said. "They said, 'We want to tease them and make sure they know Seattle is better than Portland.'"

The crowd of 8,247 at Qwest Field would be the highest attendance all season, even higher than the club's championship game against Atlanta later in the year. In fact, the attendance for the game was more than double the attendance for any other game during the 2007 season.

Arriving from France the previous day after securing his work visa, Le Toux started as an attacking center midfielder in the game. The Timbers quickly addressed Le Toux's ignorance about the rivalry in the 28th minute of the game.

Sprinting for a through-ball pass in the penalty box, Le Toux attempted to gather the ball inside the box but was leveled by Portland goalkeeper Josh Wicks. The Sounders howled for a foul and penalty kick, but referee Ian Anderson didn't agree.

Le Toux and the Sounders went on to win the game 1–0 on a goal by Nathan Knox in the 20th minute. His debut wasn't noteworthy, but Le Toux asserted himself in the rivalry when the scene shifted to Portland in the second of the home-and-home series six days later.

The crowd at PGE Park was smaller (5,722) than at Qwest Field, but just as noisy and a bit more raucous.

"The crowd was very big even though it was USL," Le Toux said. "It was almost packed on this side [pointing to the north end where the Timbers Army sits]."

Receiving a pass from Roger Levesque, Le Toux nearly scored early in the game, but his 20-yard shot sailed wide of the near post. Le Toux got another chance when Levesque lofted a perfect pass over the defense and the ball found a streaking Le Toux in stride. Le Toux was one-on-one with the hard-charging Wicks, but Le Toux cheekily chipped the ball over Wicks and into the empty net in the 8th minute.

Le Toux's goal in the game was his first as a Sounder, and he scored another goal against the Timbers in Seattle's 2–0 win on August 1, but it wouldn't be his last in 2007. He went on to score 10 goals during the regular season, helping the Sounders win the First Division title. He was named most valuable player and selected to the All-League first team.

Le Toux scored 14 goals during the regular season in 2008. He helped the Sounders eliminate two MLS teams and reach the semifinals of the U.S. Open Cup by scoring 5 goals—including 4 goals in a 6–0 win against Hollywood United—in the tournament.

Le Toux signed an MLS contract on May 8, 2008, becoming the first player the Sounders signed to an MLS contract after Seattle was awarded an MLS franchise to begin play in 2009. The Sounders were joining MLS, and Le Toux was coming along for the ride.

SCOT THOMPSON

The opposing player was a close friend, but all Thompson saw was an opponent wearing a hated Sounders jersey.

"I don't like having all this balled-up aggression and fierceness inside of me, and it always seems to come out when we play Seattle," Thompson told the *Oregonian* the day before the Sounders 1–0 win on August 6, 2008. "It's not just another game."

The bald-headed guy with "one *t*" at the end of his first name made his move on Seattle midfielder Josh Gardner, a friend and former teammate, during the game on August 7, 2008. It was the final game between the two clubs before Seattle moved on to MLS.

With Gardner making a run down the sideline, Thompson leveled Gardner with a hard—but late—tackle in the 38th minute. Referee Jasen Anno didn't hesitate, immediately pulling the red card out of his pocket.

Thompson was gone. The fans booed.

Thompson's aggressive and hard-nosed style, along with his constant hustle, quickly made him a fan favorite in Portland.

"Scot wore his heart on his sleeve. He truly cared about the organization and wanted success for himself and the organization," said Gavin Wilkinson, who played with and coached Thompson. "He reveled in the spotlight. He appreciated being adored by the fans in general. He gave back just as much."

Defender Scot Thompson played for the First Division Timbers for seven seasons (2004–10). *Photo courtesy of the Portland Timbers.*

Thompson and Gardner were teammates on the Los Angeles Galaxy in 2004, but the two found themselves on the opposite sides of the field during a U.S. Open Cup second-round game in 2007 in Tukwila, Washington.

Thompson said Gardner threw the ball at him and hit him in the groin during the game. An incensed Thompson picked up the ball and fired it right back at Gardner.

"He threw the ball at my crotch. It kind of set me off. I popped back up and threw the ball and hit him in the back," Thompson said. "I wasn't thinking, 'Oh, that was Josh.' I was thinking he was another guy on the field."

Friend? What friend? Gardner was wearing a Sounders jersey, and that's all Thompson needed to see when they met again in August. Thompson got his revenge, but evening the personal score came at a steep price.

"Scotty always came in hard. That's the way he played," Gardner said. "I thought that red card was a little harsh. I don't think he got me—maybe a yellow card.

"It was in the heat of the moment."

FREDY MONTERO

He scored the first goal in the Sounders' MLS franchise history and is the MLS franchise's all-time leader in goals scored and assists. But Montero is something of an enigma—a talented but moody star.

There's the Fredy Montero who scored twice against world power Chelsea in a friendly at CenturyLink Field on July 18, 2012. The Fredy Montero who scored twice in the Sounders' 3–2 win at Portland on July 10, 2011, and scored twice in a 3–1 win at Vancouver on September 24, 2011. The Fredy Montero who scored his first-ever MLS hat trick against Chivas on August 26, 2012. The Fredy Montero who has scored 4 goals in five MLS games against Portland.

Seattle forward Fredy Montero is the team's all-time leading scorer in MLS. *Anatoliy Lukich.*

"It's always good to score goals in those kind of derbies," Montero said.

Montero led or tied for the club lead in goals scored in the first three seasons of the Sounders' MLS existence. His total of 13 goals was second to Eddie Johnson for the club lead in 2012.

"Fredy's a player who has always been a goal scorer. At the end of the day, it's really not going to be much different," Seattle coach Sigi Schmid said. "That's what he's been, he's been very consistent in terms of what he produces for us year to year."

Flip the script and you'll find the Fredy Montero who has been benched for lackluster and unfocused performances. The Fredy Montero who spends too much time complaining to the referees and who is usually among the club and league leaders for fouls and receiving yellow cards.

Montero was benched for the second consecutive game before the Sounders' derby game against Vancouver on August 18, 2012, and he came off the bench in four other games during the 2012 season. Schmid insists that Montero isn't being punished; he's trying to get the mercurial star striker more focused.

"People always want to look at it as, 'Oh, he's being punished.' But that's not the case," Schmid said. "It's like, for every player, sometimes it's good to look at it from the outside. Everybody needs to sometimes sit down and watch."

Montero understands that Schmid is trying to help him reach his potential—but that doesn't mean he always enjoys the lessons.

"He's like a dad. In the family, there's always moments where you don't want to be in the house. But at the end of the day, you have to come back and sleep there. That's the same with Sigi and the team," Montero said. "You don't feel like you're doing that bad to receive those comments from him, but I know it's because he cares about me as a player."

There was even a rumor that Montero—no stranger to pouting when things aren't going his way—fought with teammate and fellow forward Eddie Johnson during a training session in 2012.

Schmid didn't deny the speculation. Montero did, sort of.

"There was never a fight. Why would that happen?" Montero said. "It's a game where you are 100 percent into it. Sometimes, things happen because you want to win. Sometimes you're frustrated, but it's nothing more than that."

Some of the "bad" Montero could be excused as the brashness of youth. But Montero can act like a brat despite his growing experience in MLS. However, Schmid said that Montero has handled the pressure well and is maturing as a person and player.

"He carries a lot of responsibility. His family is here, and he's the one who is really responsible for them. I can't think of a lot of twenty-three- or twenty-four-year-olds that are responsible for their entire family," Schmid said, "So you've gotta have a certain level of maturity to deal with that. He realizes there's a certain amount of pressure when he steps on the field to play, and he responds to that pressure. I think that shows a certain level of maturity."

JIMMY KELLY

Kelly could have easily embarked on a successful post-soccer career in politics by the time the 1975 regular season ended.

"Kelly for Mayor!"

Those were the words on the white and green—with green shamrocks—sign held by one adoring Timbers fan during Portland's 2–1 win against Seattle on July 26.

"I remember I was in a pizza parlor, and this little kid with a baseball uniform on came and said, 'Can I have your autograph?' I said, 'Sure, no problem,'" Kelly said. "I signed the autograph and then I looked behind me and the whole baseball team had lined up. I just sat there, signed autographs and talked to people.

"It was then that I realized that something was happening. I knew something was going on between me and the fans."

The growing legion of Portland fans quickly adopted the outside midfielder from Crumlin, Northern Ireland, as one of their own. A series of dazzling runs on the wing during the first-ever NASL regular season game between the Timbers and Sounders helped establish Kelly as a fan favorite with the fledgling team in 1975.

Bob Robinson of the *Oregonian* wrote on May 3, 1975, "The Portland Timbers and the 'new game in town'—soccer—are hardly out of the embryo stage but, already, the fans have found themselves a 'darling'…Little Jimmy Kelly dazzled the Sounders with his footwork."

Kelly wasn't the best player on the team or the most gifted, but his diminutive size (five-foot-six), dribbling skills and runs propelled him to the top of the Timbers' popularity chart in 1975. Kelly finished with eight assists during the season, second to Willie Anderson's nine assists.

A big part of Kelly's appeal was fans seeing someone who looked like themselves excelling on the field.

"I think I showed some people that you can be short and still be successful," Kelly said. "Willie and I used to take people on and beat people. People loved to see that. It was David and Goliath."

Kelly, who played with the Wolverhampton Wanderers during the English soccer season, spent three seasons (1975–76, 1981) in Portland. Kelly and Peter Withe, former teammates at Wolverhampton, had developed an uncanny connection during games, and the chemistry helped the Timbers score 43 goals, third in the league that season.

"We would kick the ball from the middle of the field and knock it out wide, and we would just kick the ball to Peter Withe," Kelly said. "Peter knew where to position himself. He knew where the ball was going to be played through. I knew when I was in certain positions, he knew where to be. It was just through practice that a player would know what another player is going to do."

Kelly and Withe connected on the field, but it was Kelly who connected with fans off the field. By the time the season had ended, the fans figured Kelly was bigger than the city of Portland.

"Jimmy Kelly for President!"

Taylor Graham

He wasn't sure about his future after being released by the MLS Kansas City Stars in 2004. His brother lived in Portland, so the big center back initially considered moving to Portland, but advice from an old friend and college teammate caused him to look north.

"Roger Levesque spoke very highly of the coach and the guys in Seattle," Graham said. "That was my first introduction to the Sounders."

Graham joined the 2005 Seattle squad that featured Levesque, defender Zach Scott, midfielders Andrew Gregor and Leighton O'Brien, along with goalkeeper Preston Burpo.

The Sounders lost to the Timbers 2–1 in their home opener in a game that featured 29 fouls, seven yellow cards and the ejection of Seattle midfielder Chad Brown (two yellow cards). That setback would prove to be the Sounders' only First Division home loss during the season. The Sounders struggled against their Cascadia rivals from the south during the regular season, winning once in four games in all competitions.

"Talking to the guys on the team and hearing their experiences. I knew it was special," Graham said. "Clearly the coach [Brian Schmetzer]—who grew up as a Sounders player—definitely knew about the rivalry and told us that this game was more important than others."

Graham experienced the Timbers Army for the first time in a U.S. Open Cup game on July 12, 2005.

"Our routine was to go on a team walk in the morning or the afternoon of gameday," Graham said. "Having people give you little sneers— there's Timbers Army fans all through downtown—everywhere you walk, people would see us in our Sounders gear and they would look at you a little differently.

"I knew they didn't like us."

Graham anchored a defense that conceded 25 goals (third-fewest in the division), and the group finished fourth in the USL First Division standings. Graham was named to the All-League first-team and selected as the league's defender of the year, beating out, among others, Portland's Scot Thompson.

Graham's stellar season earned him a contract with MLS's MetroStars (now the New York Red Bulls) in 2006. He was waived halfway through his second season in 2007, but he revived his connection with Seattle.

As fate would have it, the USL Sounders were scheduled to play a game in Rochester, New York, just days after his release. Graham signed with the Sounders, joined the club in Rochester and came on as a substitute for midfielder Hugo Alcaraz-Cuellar in the 77th minute of the Sounders' 1–0 win on July 3.

Graham and the 2007 club went on to win another First Division championship.

MARK PETERSON

Born and raised in Tacoma, the forward not only broke into the Sounders' starting lineup, but he also became a major star at the age of nineteen.

"For an American kid, he was way ahead of his time," said Alan Hinton, coach of the NASL Sounders from 1980 through 1982. "He was a young kid who could run and get in on the end of things."

The former Wilson High School prep star skipped college and joined the Sounders' developmental program in 1979. Peterson scored 18 goals in 34 games (regular season and playoffs) in 1980. He managed just 5 goals and 3 assists in 21 games in 1981, leading some observers to wonder if Peterson was just a one-season fluke.

He scored 19 goals with 5 assists in 31 games and was selected as the North American Player of the Year in 1982. He might be more remembered for the 2 goals he scored in the Sounders' 3–0 win against English Premier League power Manchester United that year.

"He wasn't a great dribbler or a flashy player. But he was a player who made great runs," said Jimmy McAlister, a teammate of Peterson in 1979. "He could make the best-timed near-post runs and near-post flick-on goals. A great first-time finisher.

Seattle forward Mark Peterson scored nineteen goals and was selected as the NASL's North American Player of the Year in 1982. *Photo courtesy of Frank McDonald.*

"He could score goals in any era, on any team anywhere in the world."

Peterson scored arguably Seattle's most important goal of the season against Portland in the Sounders' 1–0 win against the Timbers in the last game of the regular season, giving the Sounders the Western Division championship in 1982.

Peterson and fellow forward Peter Ward had formed a potent combination during the season. The two combined to score 35 of the Sounders' 72 goals as Seattle advanced to the Soccer Bowl before losing 1–0 to the New York Cosmos.

The NASL required clubs to have some North American–born players on the field at all times, so Hinton was thrilled to possess a homegrown player who was a bona fide star.

"He was gold dust because I was able as a coach to have a North American striker," Hinton said. "Most coaches in the NASL would never put a North American striker on the field to play. But Mark was very good."

DARLINGTON NAGBE

The Timbers' first-ever MLS SuperDraft pick was very close to starting his career about four hundred miles north of Portland in Vancouver, British Colombia.

Knowing he could be the top pick in the 2011 MLS SuperDraft, the soft-spoken player exercised a little leverage. The Hermann Trophy winner—awarded to the top collegiate player in the nation—and a member of the Akron Zips team that won the national title in 2010 sent signals that he didn't want to play in Vancouver.

"I told them that I have lived in the States my whole life, and I preferred to live in the United States," Nagbe said.

The expansion Whitecaps possessed the first pick of the 2011 MLS SuperDraft, with fellow expansion club Portland choosing second. The rumor floating around the MLS Combine in Fort Lauderdale, Florida, in the days leading up to the draft was that Nagbe wanted no part of the Whitecaps.

Teitur Thordarson, then the Whitecaps head coach, was taken aback when he was told about the rumor.

Portland midfielder/forward Darlington Nagbe jumps over a Seattle player during the Seattle at Portland game at Jeld-Wen Field on June 24, 2012. *Photo courtesy of the Portland Timbers.*

"If that's the case, I would have to think about that," Thordarson told the *Oregonian* on January 10, 2011.

There were rumors that Nagbe's mother, who is from Liberia, wouldn't be able to travel in and out of the United States if Nagbe was playing in Canada.

"It wasn't a concern for her, it was just me," Nagbe said. "Living here, growing up here and wanting to stay in the States."

The move spooked the Whitecaps. Not wanting to select a player who expressed reluctance about coming to the city, the Whitecaps used the first overall pick of the draft to select forward Omar Salgado.

So Nagbe "fell" to Portland, and the Timbers were thrilled to use their first-ever MLS SuperDraft pick to select Nagbe.

JIMMY McALISTER

McAlister eagerly anticipated the NASL's Soccer Bowl championship game against the New York Cosmos in 1977. He was also very nervous.

The Sounders' starting left back knew he would be involved in trying to slow New York forward Edson Arantes do Nascimento—aka the incomparable Pelé—arguably the greatest player to ever set foot on the pitch. The Cosmos' star-studded roster also included legends such as Franz "Der Kaiser" Beckenbauer, Giorgio Chinaglia and Carlos Alberto.

But it was Pelé who had the league's rookie of the year losing sleep at night. The local kid from Seattle didn't want to allow the Brazilian superstar to torch the Sounders' defense by scoring multiple goals.

"I was panicked," McAlister said. "You're a kid from Seattle and you're playing against all these big stars—including the biggest star in the world in Pelé. It began to creep into my mind, 'What the hell am I doing here?'"

At age thirty-seven, Pelé was past his prime in terms of physical abilities and skills that had led Brazil to three World Cup titles, but McAlister knew that even an aging Pelé was still better than the majority of players in the league.

"The biggest thing that went through my mind was, 'Please God, don't let me be the one to make a mistake,'" McAlister said. "As opposed to the guy saying, 'Hey, give me the ball and let me be the hero.'"

Pelé didn't score in the Cosmos' 2–1 win in front of 35,548 fans at Portland's Civic Stadium, but he respected the rookie's defense and hustle in the game. In appreciation of McAlister's defense, Pelé exchanged jerseys with McAlister after the game.

Sounders of the Future

WARD FORREST
Bellevue, WA

JIM MC ALISTER
Seattle, WA

DARRELL OAK
Tacoma, WA

DAVE OBERBILLIG
Bellevue, WA

MATT O'SULLIVAN
San Francisco, CA

PAUL RENKERT
Bellevue, WA

not pictured
TERRY HICKEY
Bellevue, WA

DEAN WURZBERGER
Sacramento, CA

Seattle defender Jimmy McAlister exchanged jerseys with the legendary Pelé after the Sounders lost to the New York Cosmos in the 1977 Soccer Bowl. *From 1976 Sounders Yearbook, courtesy of Russ Daggatt.*

McAlister still possesses Pelé's gift—the jersey, not the skills.

"The jersey is in my son's bank safety deposit box. I've been offered to sell it about fifteen times," McAlister said. "I've never sold it."

BYRON ALVAREZ

Just a few inches of skin separate the Timbers' logo tattooed on his chest and his heart. That's how much Bryon Alvarez loved the Timbers. But like many love affairs, the ending was bitter.

For Alvarez.

"Not being able to finish my career on the team that I gave everything to…I felt sad and angry at times," Alvarez said. "I would have really loved to have finished my career with the Timbers. I didn't, and I was mad for that."

The breakup wasn't what Alvarez expected after pouring his heart and soul into the Timbers, especially during his first season with the club in 2003.

Alvarez signed with the Timbers and started playing, but he didn't have a visa. Without a visa, Alvarez didn't get paid, but he played his heart out the entire season despite persistent financial issues.

"My work permit had expired, so I wasn't able to get paid by the club. I was playing practically for free," Alvarez said. "I would train and then I would do some work on the side after practice. That's how I survived."

Alvarez didn't score in the first eight games of the 2003 season, but when he finally scored his first goal in the ninth game, the floodgates opened. Alvarez scored 11 goals in the final 20 games—including a 2-goal performance in a 3–1 win against Seattle on August 9—and led the club in goals, with 12.

"They wanted to break my legs. Their defenders wanted to do everything to me, and I realized that there was something going on between Seattle and Portland," Alvarez said. "Every time I played against them, I would bring everything—my guns, knife, whatever I needed to do battle."

Alvarez produced his best season in 2004, scoring 16 goals—including a hat trick in the Timbers' 6–0 home win against Edmonton June 10—during the season. Alvarez scored 3 goals against Seattle in the regular season and playoffs. Alvarez was selected to the All-League first team, helping the Timbers post the best record in the regular season.

That magical season proved to be the highlight of Alvarez's first four seasons with the Timbers. Alvarez scored 9 goals in 2005 and then scored just 4 goals under new coach Chris Agnello in 2006. Agnello was fired after the Timbers finished with their worst record (7–15–6, 27 points), since joining the USL.

Gavin Wilkinson was named as coach and general manager in 2007 after Merritt Paulson purchased the franchise. But stars Alvarez, Alan Gordon and Andrew Gregor didn't re-sign with the Timbers. Alvarez's 41 goals left him as the Timbers' modern franchise all-time leading goal scorer.

Alvarez signed with Charleston, where his career fizzled, and he reunited with Wilkinson in July 2008. Wilkinson offered Alvarez a chance to play in the Timbers' friendly against Mexico's UANL Tigres on July 15. The Timbers had been struggling to score goals in league play and needed help.

"When he came back on trial for us, he was motivated. He played very well, and he looked very sharp in training," Wilkinson said. "You make a decision based on the player that you knew, the person and the player that you saw."

Alvarez scored a goal and added an assist in the Timbers' 2–0 win and signed with the club for the remainder of the 2008 season. Alvarez scored 1 goal in 9 appearances and parted ways with the Timbers for the final time.

"We were having a tremendous problem scoring. We brought him back in to try and help the situation," Wilkinson said. "It didn't pan out as we would have liked."

The trial was a decision Alvarez would do differently if he had a second chance.

"At that point in my career, I had nothing to prove," Alvarez said. "I don't think I needed to prove that I can score goals. I have been doing that all my life."

ROGER DAVIES

A one-season wonder?

That would be the easy description of the forward who made coach Alan Hinton look like a genius—for one season. The first-year coach, hired by Seattle after being fired in Tulsa, wanted to acquire Davies despite Davies's rather pedestrian performance—8 goals and 7 assists in 22 appearances—during his final regular season in Tulsa in 1979.

Hinton finally got his man, trading for Davies—along with defender David Nish and goalkeeper Jack Brand—by sending forward Tommy Ord, defender Bruce Rudoff and cash to Tulsa in December 1979. The six-foot-two, 190-pound Davies blitzed the league with 25 goals in 29 appearances and added 11 assists in 1980.

"Having played with Alan and then to play for him in Tulsa, Seattle was easy because of the relationship I had and still have with him," Davies said. "[Hinton] would tell me to get myself in the box, and he would make sure the supply would come and it did."

He scored 9 game-winning goals and scored 4 goals in a game against Rochester, displaying an ability to score in a variety—header, right-footed shot and 2 goals with his left foot—of ways.

Seattle forward Roger Davies scored 25 goals and added 11 assists in 29 games in 1980. He was selected as the NASL's most valuable player. *Photo courtesy of Frank McDonald.*

"I was so full of confidence," Davies said. "I felt I would score every game. It does not happen very often in a career, but for me, I felt great."

Davies led the Sounders to a 25–7 record, the best regular season mark in NASL history and was voted the league's most valuable player. That season turned out to be the high point of Davies's NASL career as injuries began to take a toll on his feet and knees.

His boots were slit on the side to relieve pressure on his swollen feet. He often received pain-killing injections before games. And the artificial turf back in the day was unforgiving.

"It was an old injury that just came back," Davies said. "Maybe Astro [Turf] did not help."

The first of a series of knee problems surfaced after the 1980 season and limited Davies to 6 goals and 5 assists in 23 games in 1981. Knee surgery snuffed out nearly his entire 1982 season—he played in just 12 regular season games.

"After such a great season it was terrible not being able to play," Davies said. "The knee never really recovered fully, but it has not stopped me from still playing."

JOHN BAIN

During the last game of the 1978 season, he posted a first. Bain scored 3 goals in the Timbers' 3–1 win at Colorado on August 2, becoming the first Portland player in franchise history to hit the back of the net three times in a game. The end-of-the-season performance marked the beginning of an impressive goal-scoring career for the native of Glasgow, Scotland.

Bain's career at Bristol City hit a wall in England at the age of twenty, and when the opportunity surfaced to play in the NASL, Bain quickly agreed to join Portland on loan in 1978.

"Initially, I was coming over to get experience. I was on the first-team squad, but not playing in a lot of games. At that point in my career, I felt it was a good move for me," Bain said. "But my thought was always to go back to England and play. I always thought this was going to be a stepping stone."

The rookie scored 6 goals and added 3 assists in 25 appearances during the regular season. The five-foot-eight Bain scored the winning goal in overtime of the Timbers' win against Washington, helping the Timbers advance into the NASL playoff conference semifinals. Bain then delivered the assist on Willie Anderson's game and series–winning goal in the semifinals against Vancouver to propel the Timbers to the NASL conference championship series, where they lost to New York.

John Bain finished his five-year NASL career in Portland as the franchise's all-time leader in goals, assists and points. He later played one season with the Sounders. *Photo courtesy of the* Oregonian.

Bain's 8 goals tied him with Clyde Best as the team leader, and his 11 assists tied him with Willie Anderson for the team lead in that statistical category in 1979. Bain flourished in his final three seasons in Portland, reaching double digits in assists in each season and scoring at least 10 goals in two of the three seasons. Bain scored 11 goals and added 12 assists in 1981, helping the Timbers reach the playoffs. Bain finished his career as the NASL Timbers' all-time leader in points (145), goals (45) and assists (55).

And the only player to achieve a hat trick.

MARCUS HAHNEMANN

When he stepped inside the net as the Sounders' goalkeeper against CD Marathon on October 24, 2012, his career had come full circle.

"This is where I started my career, and I wanted to finish here," Hahnemann said.

The start against the Honduran club in a CONCACAF Champions League game was his first game in a Sounders uniform since 1996, when he was a member of Seattle's A-League championship clubs. The game also represented his first competitive action since he was in net for Wolverhampton in a 1–0 loss to Stoke City in England's FA Cup tournament on January 30, 2011.

Hahnemann wasn't sure he would get another opportunity to play at a high level professionally during the summer of 2012, when the then forty-year-old was released by EPL club Everton in May. He returned to Seattle and shifted into retirement mode after an eighteen-year career in which he played in the English Premier League and nine international games with the U.S. National Team.

Yet Hahnemann held out hope that he would sign with Seattle. Rumors of Hahnemann returning to Seattle had surfaced in the past. There were reports that the Sounders were interested in Hahnemann after Kasey Keller retired following the 2011 season, but general manager Adrian Hanauer said the MLS allocation process was a significant obstacle.

"When it looked like I wasn't going to get a chance to play again for the Sounders and be a part of it, it was pretty frustrating," Hahnemann said. "I thought I really missed out."

The Sounders, through the allocation process, traded a conditional draft pick to Toronto FC to acquire Hahnemann and signed him on September 14, 2012.

Seattle goalkeeper Marcus Hahnemann led the Sounders to two consecutive A-League titles in 1995 and 1996. *Photo courtesy of Frank McDonald.*

"I had resigned myself to the fact that I wasn't going to be playing for the Sounders again. That was pretty disappointing," Hahnemann said. "All of a sudden, to be given that second chance to come back, it's absolutely amazing."

The Sounders didn't sign Hahnemann as a public relations stunt: they saw him eventually ascending to the backup role behind Michael Gspurning.

"I would say it was all soccer. We wouldn't have done it for sentiment," Seattle general manager Adrian Hanauer told SoundersFC.com. "We think he's still got good goalkeeping in him. It's always an added bonus when there's a little bit of sentiment there, but we're in the business of winning championships. If he couldn't do the business, we wouldn't have signed him."

That's why the former Seattle Pacific University star started in the game against CD Marathon, and his performance in that game caused the Sounders to change their thinking about Hahnemann's future.

WILLIE ANDERSON

Anderson remembers chatting with former Aston Villa teammate Brian Godfrey over a post-game beer in April 1975.

"He said to me, off the cuff, 'Guess what I'm doing this summer?'" Anderson recalled. "I said, 'I have no idea.' And he said, 'I'm gonna go play in America!'"

Anderson didn't really need to play during England's off-season; he was an established star at Aston Villa before signing with Cardiff City in 1973. Anderson had scored 36 goals in 231 appearances with Aston Villa from 1967 to 1973 and scored 12 goals in 126 appearances with Cardiff City.

Portland midfielder Willie Anderson played for seven seasons with the NASL Timbers. He finished his career as the franchise leader in games played, was second in assists and fourth in points scored. *Photo courtesy of the Portland Timbers.*

"Brian told me Vic Crowe was the coach, and I played for Vic Crowe at Aston Villa. I told Brian if Vic was looking for players, I would be interested," Anderson said. "Later I talked to Vic about it, and Vic put a deal together with Cardiff City."

Anderson didn't know where the state of Oregon was, but he wasn't going to let that minor detail prevent him and his family from making their first trip to the States.

"I looked at it as a paid vacation for myself and my family to come over to America for four months to play as well as see America," Anderson said.

Crowe, who had been in the state for all of about two months, provided some clues about living in Oregon.

"I remember Vic telling me it was next to California. So I said, 'The weather must be great.' And he said, 'Yeah, just like California,'" Anderson said. "The first two weeks I was here, it rained every day."

By the time all the details were finished, Anderson arrived for Portland's road game at Vancouver, the fourth game of the season. Anderson was delayed by his commitment to Cardiff City's run in the 1975 Welsh Cup tournament.

The five-foot-eight Anderson didn't experience any issues on the field, displaying the ability to get by defenders. Anderson, at the right midfielder position, was the perfect complement to the left-footed Jimmy Kelly on the left side.

"He was a nightmare to play against. He was quick, and he had an uncanny ability to keep you unsettled as a defender," said defender Mick Hoban, who saw plenty of Anderson during training sessions. "Think of it like a wide receiver against a cornerback. You never knew if he was going to stop short or go beyond you.

"Willie was good with either foot, so you didn't know if he was going inside you or outside you. Once he had made his move, his first couple of steps were so quick, that he was by you. Once he was gone, all you could see was the back of his jersey."

Anderson (nine assists) and Kelly (eight assists) were able to send plenty of crosses to the "Wizard of Nod," Peter Withe, who scored 17 goals during the regular season and playoffs.

"You put two wings out there—Jimmy and myself—and our job was to cross the ball into the box so Peter could do something," Anderson said. "Peter was a big striker who was great with his heading ability."

Anderson had so much fun and enjoyed life in the Rose City so much that he wasn't eager to return to England. Cardiff City had loaned Anderson to the Timbers, and the Bluebirds were anxious for the winger to return to Wales. But the Timbers were finishing up an incredible inaugural NASL season and had earned a berth in the playoffs.

Anderson eventually returned to Cardiff City and played for the club during the 1975–76 season, but Cardiff manager Jimmy Andrews, still miffed at Anderson's late return, refused to allow him to play for the Timbers in 1976. Anderson returned to the Timbers after signing a contract in 1977.

"I made a ton of great friends, and I just loved the American lifestyle," Anderson said. "I just got here and I thought, 'I want to live here.' It was that quick for me."

MICK HOBAN

He knew he was coming to Portland to do more than just play soccer. Hoban had to sell a sport to the uninformed masses. The NASL had just awarded a professional soccer franchise to Portland, a city where most residents knew very little about the sport.

"We had to spread the gospel of soccer," Hoban said. "It wasn't a matter of just introducing the Timbers, we had to introduce the game."

Hoban was one of the first two—Brian Godfrey was the other—players signed by the expansion franchise. Hoban was already NASL-savvy by the time he arrived in Portland as the first Timbers player to set foot in the city. Hoban had played in Atlanta and Denver between 1971 and 1974 before coming to Portland and had also been each club's liason between the franchise and the community.

"In England, I was a reserve team player and on the fringe of the first team. I was sent to the States in 1971 to get that experience," Hoban said. "I was struck by the magnitude of the country and the fact that you had to fly to games and the fact that you were playing in these massive stadiums that weren't made for soccer. When I went back home, I knew I wanted a piece of that."

Hoban, twenty years old at the time, was sent out to help fans learn about the game, promote the game and help foreign players adjust to living in the United States. He took on the same role when he joined the Timbers.

"There were lots of pretty basic questions about the game, the coach that was coming here or certain players," Hoban said. "There were questions about the game itself. People would ask questions about offside, systems or formations. People would ask me about our strategy against the Sounders."

Hoban received some help when the Timbers signed more players in the coming weeks. Those players were also expected to fan out into the city and create a buzz about the new club.

"You got to meet Americans and go into schools, coaching seminars and stuff like that," midfielder Willie Anderson said. "We understood it was part of playing and helping grow the team."

The city warmed up to the new sport. The Timbers drew 8,131 fans to their season-opening game against Seattle and averaged more than 32,500 for their two playoff games at the end of the season.

"It was almost like a perfect storm of things that came together," Hoban said. "The need for a second professional sports franchise in town. The cost of tickets being reasonable. Family orientation and a successful team on the field as the team got going.

"And we started winning games all the way to the Soccer Bowl."

Chapter 4

THE COACHES

John Best

A romantic relationship of potential and promise between the expansion Sounders and the Seattle-area fans quickly developed in 1974.

With fans having little knowledge about the sport, the Sounders drew 12,132 to the first-ever home game on May 12, 1974.

"Most of the players had been playing in the second division or the third division in Great Britain. We were used to playing in front of a couple thousand people, and they didn't cheer for us very often," Best said. "When we played the first game at home, we were expecting about 2,500 to 3,000 people. And we got about 13,000 people. It was unbelievable."

The club wasn't a one-game wonder. They drew a sell-out crowd of 13,876 for their 2–0 win against Philadelphia on June 22, the first sell-out crowd in NASL history.

Best, who had played briefly in the Liverpool FC system and later with the Tranmere Rovers, a smaller club near Liverpool, enjoyed success as a player with the NASL's Dallas Tornado. Best was a five-time all-star with the Tornado and helped the club win the NASL championship in 1971 before retiring in 1973.

Seattle managing partner Walt Daggatt and the Sounders zeroed in on Best after Dallas owner Lamar Hunt recommended Best to the club.

"I think the commissioner was involved, and Lamar had also talked to some people in the Sounders organization," Best said. "The Sounders called

John Best (left) coached the Sounders for three seasons (1974–76) before he was succeeded by Jimmy Gabriel (right). *Photo courtesy of Frank McDonald.*

Dallas for permission to talk to me. I met Walt and some of the other owners and they offered me the job."

Best guided the Sounders to a 10–7–3 record and a third-place finish (behind the Los Angeles Aztecs and San Jose) in the Western Division in their inaugural season. They conceded a league-low 17 goals and accumulated—in the NASL's convoluted scoring system—101 points, fifth-highest in the league.

The Sounders didn't quality for the playoffs, due to the NASL's strange qualifying system (two division winners, plus teams with highest overall point total in each conference).

"We had more points than just about everybody in the other division," Best said. "They changed the playoff format after that, so if one conference was much stronger than the other, they allowed that conference to have more teams qualify."

The Sounders didn't make the playoffs in 1974, but their success at the gate during the inaugural season prompted an expansion of seating at Memorial Stadium prior to the 1975 season. Seating capacity at the stadium increased from 12,000 to 17,925, and the Sounders drew more fans.

The Sounders defeated the Timbers 1–0 in the season opener, which began the expansion Timbers' inaugural season. Best and the Sounders finished second behind the Timbers, who amassed the most points in the league during the regular season. The two clubs met in the playoff quarterfinal game that Best described as memorable.

"I'll never forget coming out of the tunnel how the crowd was so loud and it was packed. They added additional bleachers on the side opposite the player tunnel," Best said. "Beyond that, there were people outside of the stadium sitting in trees, looking out of windows. You saw people going anywhere they could to get a view of the game.

"It so much reminded me of similar games in England. It was amazing."

VIC CROWE

The hard-nosed coach made it clear from the get-go: Don't expect me to be all warm and fuzzy. I'm not going to be your buddy. I'm your coach.

"He didn't want to be your best friend, and he knew you would never be his best friend," midfielder Willie Anderson said. "He was straight upfront. He would look you in the face and say, 'Hey, I'm leaving you out [of the lineup] because you're playing like crap.'"

As a youth, Mick Hoban saw Crowe as a player at Aston Villa and was a member of the Aston Villa club when Crowe was the coach.

"I sort of likened him to [Chicago Bears' Hall of Fame linebacker] Dick Butkus. A no-nonsense defensive type," Hoban said. "That's how he was as a manager. A highly disciplined, well-organized, focused and competitive coach. Every practice was run with military-style discipline."

Crowe wasn't the Timbers' first choice to manage the expansion squad in 1975. General manager Don Paul wanted another Englishman, Gordon Jago, because of his previous experience as coach of the NASL's Baltimore

Portland coach Vic Crowe laughs it up with a "tree" before a game. *Photo courtesy of the Oregonian.*

Bays. Jago was coaching Millwall in Southeast London, but Paul and the club couldn't agree on buyout terms. Crowe also played with the Atlanta Chiefs of the NASL for three seasons and was familiar with the league.

Crowe didn't use the lack of training time as an excuse for a lack of quality in the first game against Seattle. The training sessions were often more grueling than the games.

"If anyone thought we were coming over here just to play for three months, go out and party and have a good time, they were mistaken," Hoban said. "We worked our asses off in training."

Fitness and maintaining fitness was never far from Crowe's thinking, even when the Timbers traveled to away games.

"There was an old saying about Vic, 'We never passed a hill that we wouldn't run up,'" midfielder Jimmy Kelly said.

Even though Crowe is remembered as a stone-faced, no-nonsense, drill sergeant type of coach, he did possess a lighter side that occasionally surfaced. Kelly recalled that Crowe's dry sense of humor sometimes caught others by surprise.

"Things would happen, and you could see his shoulders going up and down, laughing. Just stupid little things that would go on in everyday life," Kelly said. "He thought it was funny, but a lot of players would ask me, 'What's he laughing about?' Nobody else would think it was funny but Vic."

Alan Hinton

The coach seemingly could do no wrong during his first season in Seattle. His squad set an NASL record for regular season wins. He acquired Roger Davies, who scored an astounding 25 goals in 29 games. He guided the team to the Soccer Bowl.

The Sounders looked past Hinton's turbulent season with the Tulsa Roughnecks and decided he was the right man to replace Jimmy Gabriel in 1980.

The Roughnecks didn't have any star players on the roster and operated with one of the smallest payrolls in the league. The franchise had trouble meeting the payroll on a number of occasions, causing strife within the locker room.

"The club had some financial issues. I actually came down on the side of the players, and I lost my job," Hinton said. "It didn't affect the performance on the field because we did very well. That's why the Sounders hired me, because of my record at Tulsa."

Hinton guided the Roughnecks to a mediocre regular season record (14–16, there were no ties), and the club posted an average attendance of 16,426 a game (sixth in the NASL) in 1979. Hinton and the Roughnecks performed very well in the playoffs, reaching the two-game conference semifinal against the vaunted and star-studded New York Cosmos.

The two clubs split the first two games, winning by 3–0 scores. The Cosmos advanced by defeating the Roughnecks 3–1 in a "mini-game."

"They had this stupid mini-game, fifteen minutes each way," Hinton said. "We went to a shootout, and we got beat in the shootout. If the rules had been more modern, we would've gone through."

Hinton was well aware of Davies before he arrived in Seattle. The two were teammates at England's Derby County for six seasons (1971–76) before reuniting in Tulsa. Tulsa wasn't interested in Davies after injuries limited him to 22 games in 1979.

Seattle coach Alan Hinton led the Sounders to a then NASL all-time-best record of 25–7 and the Soccer Bowl in 1980. *Photo courtesy of Frank McDonald.*

"Roger was a very talented player. I saw that when we were back in England," Hinton said. "I played with him at Derby County. I knew what he could do."

Hinton acquired Davies—and defender David Nish and goalkeeper Jack Brand—and sent forward Tommy Ord, defender Bruce Rudoff and cash to Tulsa in December 1979.

Hinton's first season in Seattle was a major success as the Sounders roared through the regular season with a 25–7 record (no ties) and they swept the two-game season series against Portland by identical 1–0 scores. The Sounders finished second in the league in points (207), third in goals scored (74) and first in goals conceded (31).

Davies added 11 assists to his 25 goals and was named the league's most valuable player. Brand was the league's best goalkeeper, and Hinton was selected as coach of the year.

"Roger was a big guy who was very good in the air offensively and defensively," Hinton said. "He had really quick feet for a big guy, and he knew how to score."

The Sounders won two consecutive games to defeat Vancouver in the first round of the playoffs. They split the two games against Los Angeles in the conference semifinals, but the NASL's mini-game tiebreaker system once again haunted Hinton. The Aztecs won the shortened third game 2–1 to advance to the conference final.

Beset by complaints from Hinton (about the referees), some players (about Hinton), the fans (about the team) and injuries, the Sounders slumped to a fourth-place finish (15–17) in the regular season in the Northwest Division and were bounced out of the playoffs in the first round by Chicago in 1981.

Hinton and the Sounders reestablished themselves with another run at the championship the following season.

Led by forwards Peter Ward (18 goals, 12 assists before being selected most valuable player) and local product Mark Peterson (17 goals), along with setup midfielder Steve Daley (18 assists), the Sounders finished first in the Western Division (18–14).

They advanced to the NASL championship game to face the Cosmos. The Sounders had a chance to avenge their loss in the 1977 Soccer Bowl, and Hinton had an opportunity for revenge after his Tulsa squad was ousted by the Cosmos in the 1979 conference semifinals.

Instead, Hinton and the Sounders' frustration would continue, losing 1–0.

DON MEGSON

What was it about Timbers coaches and their first season? Megson, brought in after Brian Tiler's disastrous season (10–16) in 1977, experienced similar success to Crowe in his first season. Megson guided the Timbers to the NASL conference semifinals before losing to the Cosmos in his first season in 1978.

"He was set in his ways. Coaches at Don's age are set in their ways," said midfielder John Bain. "They're old-fashioned about how they look at the game."

Megson walked into a mess after Tiler's first and only season (the Timbers lost nine of their final twelve games) as coach and promptly cleaned house. Megson re-signed nine of the twenty players on the 1977 roster. Willie Anderson, Clyde Best, Graham Day, Brian Gant, Mick Hoban, Ike MacKay, Mick Poole, Archie Robostoff and Stewart Scullion all returned for the 1978 season.

Hoban, a player in the Aston Villa youth system when Vic Crowe was coach and who had been with the Timbers since the expansion season, said he didn't see much difference between the styles and philosophies of Megson and Crowe.

Don Megson coached the Timbers for two full seasons (1978, 1979), before he was fired during the 1980 season. *Photo courtesy of the* Oregonian.

"Don was cut from the same cloth as Vic," Hoban said. "He was a very talented, uncompromising and hard-nosed defender. That's the way he was as a player, and his coaching style was the same."

Megson, a longtime defender for Sheffield Wednesday, took a similar approach as Crowe to fill out the roster. Megson traveled back to his native England to find players who fit into his system. Megson signed a few players who later became legends with the Timbers.

Megson signed Bain, the Scottish striker who would eventually finish his career in Portland as the franchise's all-time leader in goals, assists and points. Megson also signed Clive Charles. Charles made his name in youth and college soccer in the Portland metropolitan area. Midfielder Jimmy Conway came to the Timbers from Manchester City in 1978. The Irish international was named the Timbers' player/coach under Megson before the 1980 season.

Bain, Charles and Conway have all been inducted into the Timbers' Ring of Honor.

BRIAN SCHMETZER

The triumphant feeling of conqueror enveloped Brian Schmetzer after the referee blew his whistle to end the game. The Sounders had beaten the Timbers for the second consecutive game in the 2005 playoffs and knocked Portland out of the playoffs for the second consecutive season.

"We just didn't like each other," Schmetzer said. "When you sit there and you play professional sports, yes, it's a job, but there's certain teams that you may not particularly care for."

Schmetzer was the Sounders' coach during those playoff wins, but his experience in the rivalry dates back three decades. Born and raised in Seattle, Schmetzer was an outstanding forward at Nathan Hale High before joining the NASL Sounders in 1980. He was around for the final two seasons of the rivalry before the Timbers folded after the 1982 season.

Schmetzer played in plenty of reserve team games between the two clubs. The intensity of the rivalry in those reserve games was no less than in the first team games.

"We're playing for our lives. It was our livelihood and our jobs," Schmetzer said. "The games, even though they were reserve games, were very spirited and tough matches."

Schmetzer was hired as coach of the Sounders' A-League club in 2002. And his first win as coach came against the Timbers in a U.S. Open Cup qualifying game in May 2002. And the win occurred in hostile territory—8,775 mostly Portland fans watched in horror as the Sounders walked out with a 2–0 win at PGE Park.

"The number one thing with Brian is he built a family of players," said Darren Sawatzky, who played for Schmetzer in 2000 and 2002–04. "That's the atmosphere that Brian helped create. In it together."

Not only did the win come against the archrival, but Schmetzer also beat his mentor Bobby Howe, who was the coach of the Timbers at the time.

"It was a win, and it was against someone I considered had much more experience than I did," Schmetzer said. "That was a very satisfying win for me."

Schmetzer said he will not forget the fans in Portland. Schmetzer loves the Seattle fans, but those Timbers fans—particularly the Timbers Army—have always possessed a unique ability to attract attention, sometimes to the point of being irritating.

"The Timbers Army might be a little rougher around the edges. They're very adamant about their support for their team," Schmetzer said. "I think that helped the rivalry, because you have groups that are so passionate about their respective teams. That always leads to the inevitable altercations and moments in time where things can happen that makes news."

Quieting the Timbers Army, especially in playoff competition, ranks as one of Schmetzer's highlights as a coach.

"We didn't like the Timbers, and it always felt good to beat them," Schmetzer said.

BOBBY HOWE

How ironic. The man who played for Seattle watches his coaching career in Portland end with…a loss to the Sounders in the playoffs.

"We had such a fantastic run into the end of the season, we thought this could be our year. The regular season hadn't gone so well, we turned it around and we had momentum on our side," Howe said. "We had done an unbelievable job of turning our season around just to get into the playoffs. Being knocked out in the playoffs was very disappointing, especially losing to Seattle."

The loss to the Sounders was the last straw for then Timbers president John Cunningham, who announced in a written statement that Howe had been "relieved of his duties" on October 11, 2005—one month after the Timbers lost to the Sounders in the playoffs for the second consecutive season.

Howe, who had guided the Timbers to the playoffs in four of his five seasons, said he was surprised by the decision and indicated the dismissal was more finance-related than based on performance.

"The bottom line is the club lost money," Howe said.

Howe's dismissal ended an era for one of the primary individuals involved in the return of soccer to Portland in 2001 after an eleven-year absence.

"It was a baseball and soccer operation, and it changed hands a couple of times," Howe said. "One of the reasons that soccer continued was the sport was riding the coattails of baseball. They were tied together. They needed a soccer team to be able to operate the baseball team in the stadium."

The former West Ham defender had retired from playing in England in 1974. He wanted to remain close to the game as a coach, but nothing suitable presented itself until an old friend from his days in England contacted him.

Jimmy Gabriel was named to succeed John Best as coach of the Sounders in 1977. Gabriel asked Howe and Harry Redknapp—all three were club players at Bournemouth in the early to mid-1970s—to join him in the dual capacity of player/assistant coach. However, the term "player" was rarely mentioned in the same sentence with Howe's name. He appeared in all of 11 games during his seven seasons with the Sounders.

"The NASL season started before the league seasons had ended in Europe. Consequently, we were always waiting for players to come over and start playing for the Sounders," Howe said. "I only played for the Sounders in those periods in April or May, whenever our league started at that time before the other players came over."

Howe was out of a job when the Sounders folded in 1983. He took a position with the U.S. Soccer Federation, but he wanted to coach. A teammate from his West Ham days—Clive Charles—told him about an investment group that had formed a professional soccer club in Portland and was searching for a coach.

"I wasn't totally excited about the role I had at the U.S. Soccer Federation, and the opportunity presented itself for me to coach the Portland Timbers," Howe said. "I was really interested to get back into coaching with a pro team again."

Howe finished his five-year coaching career in Portland with a winning record, but his playoff record against Seattle led to his dismissal.

Neil Megson

Call him the Rodney Dangerfield of Seattle coaches. The son of former Portland coach Don Megson says he doesn't get any respect from the Sounders for his work and dedication to the franchise during the Sounders' era between the NASL and the USL. Megson claims that no one wishes to acknowledge the A-League's contribution to the rise of professional soccer in the United States.

"I think what we did was we kept it going to what it has become today. It hasn't gotten as much recognition as it should have," Megson said. "If it wasn't for the A-League, the MLS would never have been there."

Megson, who followed Alan Hinton as coach of the squad in 1996 (he was also a player), managed to win an A-League championship despite his club being raided by newly formed Major League Soccer.

"We knew the MLS was coming in, and they basically took a third of the best players in the A-League. And then they just left us," Megson said. "They didn't give us any compensation for the players. We nurtured along those players and then they just took the players, left and basically just shut the door and didn't say thanks."

Megson said his success didn't impress the Sounders management enough to acknowledge his contribution to the franchise.

"They have never considered me in a role of helping the academy, reserves or the head coaching position," Megson said. "They had their own agenda, they are going to stick to it and they're going to do what they're going to do."

Megson credited Bobby Howe for helping him as a player and Hinton, not his father, for mentoring him and teaching him about coaching.

"Alan Hinton had a bigger influence on my coaching career because he was close by and it was convenient," Megson said. "He held no grudge that I got the job after him. I think he was the one who recommended me for the job."

Megson, a star player at Lake Oswego High School in Oregon, opted to remain in the United States after his father returned to England. He spent one season with the NASL Sounders in 1983, the club's final year in the NASL.

Megson says he simply wants some recognition for the A-League itself, along with the players, coaches and owners who helped the sport remain afloat in the Pacific Northwest.

"It left a bad taste in many players' mouths—the guys who had a career in the A-League but did not get a chance to prove themselves in MLS," Megson said. "If it wasn't for the A-League, the MLS may not be where it is today."

GAVIN WILKINSON

He was passed over for the head coach position in favor of Chris Agnello in 2005 but received his chance less than a year later. Wilkinson was still on the active roster as a defender—he appeared in eight games—and assistant coach when Agnello resigned immediately after the Timbers posted a 7–15–6 record and finished in a tie for last place in the USL First Division in 2006.

Agnello's decision caught then president John Cunningham by surprise. A scrambling Cunningham took less than a week to name Wilkinson as the new coach.

Wilkinson cleared out nearly the entire team in a reshuffling of the roster. Eyebrows were raised when stars Hugo Alcaraz-Cuellar and Byron Alvarez did not re-sign with the team.

"We couldn't afford to keep them with where we were at that stage. The organization was struggling," Wilkinson said. "We had one of the smallest budgets in the league to put out a quality product on the field. With Hugo, would we have loved to have kept him? Definitely. We just couldn't afford him."

The shakeup worked. Wilkinson instilled a defensive mindset, and the Timbers cut down on the goals conceded, allowing a division-leading 18 goals

Gavin Wilkinson has been with the Timbers since 2001 as a player, assistant coach, head coach and general manager. *Photo courtesy of the Portland Timbers.*

in 2007, compared to 39 in 2006. The Timbers were winless against Seattle (0–2–1), but they completed the season with a 14–5–9 record and finished in second place. They defeated Vancouver on aggregate goals in the first round of the playoffs before losing to Atlanta on penalty kicks in the semifinals.

Wilkinson—under pressure from new owner Merritt Paulson, who purchased the team from California businessman Abe Alizadah in May 2007—cleaned house again after a dismal last place finish in 2008. Another roster purge, another successful regular season. This time Wilkinson focused on revamping the offense after scoring a division-low 26 goals in 2008. The Timbers led the division in goals scored (45), tied for goals allowed (19) and set an all-time First Division record with a 24-game unbeaten streak. The streak was quickly forgotten when Vancouver eliminated the Timbers on aggregate goals in the two-leg semifinal.

SIGI SCHMID

It took less than five minutes for the Sounders coach to transform what was a rather ordinary 1–1 draw into a nasty exchange that elevated the rivalry into the MLS era.

Schmid didn't throw any compliments toward the Timbers during his post-game comments after the first-ever MLS regular season game in the rivalry on May 14, 2011.

"I think the weather suited them a little bit more," Schmid said.

Huh? Uh, coach, doesn't it rain more often in Seattle than in Portland?

In fact, many fans in Portland said the Seattle coach came across as condescending toward the Timbers' effort in the game.

"Their game is predicated around free kicks and set pieces," Schmid said. "That's what their danger is. That's what they live for. The referee gave them quite a few."

Schmid insisted he wasn't devaluing the Timbers' talent, but Portland coach John Spencer took offense. The emotional Spencer didn't mention Schmid by name, but he ripped into Schmid's comments two days after the game.

"I think if it is too wet up there for them to play soccer then they may want to move that franchise because it pisses down rain nearly every time I've been in Seattle. Obviously, to say that the conditions suit us more than they suit them just blows me away. It seems to me they had fifty excuses before the game written down as to why they never beat us three or four-nil at home," Spencer said. "The next time we go up there we'll take plenty of

Seattle head coach Sigi Schmid wasn't happy during the Sounders' 2–1 loss at Portland's Jeld-Wen Field on June 24, 2012, but the Sounders defeated the Timbers 3–0 at CenturyLink Field on October 7, 2012. *Anatoliy Lukich.*

towels for them so we can dry off the field before the game. Maybe take plenty of tissue paper so they can dry their eyes after the game."

Schmid tried to put the controversy behind him when the two teams met again later in the season on July 10 at Jeld-Wen Field in Portland.

"I have no issues with John Spencer. There's no hard feelings," Schmid said. "Maybe that disappoints people."

Schmid also attempted to explain the difference in style of play between the two clubs, which sounded like the Sounders played a more "true" game of soccer by emphasizing player and ball movement to attack, rather than using a direct approach of dumping the ball into the penalty box area.

"The difference is if we get a free kick from 50 yards out from goal, are we going to try to put the ball in play or we going to knock it into the 18-yard box?" Schmid said. "We might tend to put it into play a little bit more rather than knock it forward."

Regardless of what Schmid was trying to say, some fans and members within the Timbers organization took his comments as another case of the Sounders positioning themselves as not only the better club in overall talent, but also one that possesses more style on the field.

The Sounders had Schmid's back in the second game of the 2011 season.

The Sounders rallied twice from one-goal deficits in the game and scored the final two goals of the game to win 3–2. Fredy Montero scored both equalizing goals, and Osvaldo Alonso scored the game-winner on a penalty kick—Portland center back Eric Brunner fouled forward Lamar Neagle in the box—in the 83rd minute.

"You come back twice, and then you take the lead. It's a team effort…and we're certainly getting the rewards for it," goalkeeper Kasey Keller said after the game. "The team knows that we're capable of coming back in any kind of situation and we can get results out of it."

Coming off the disappointing draw and resulting controversy after the first game in May, the win was satisfying for the Sounders—and hugely deflating for the Timbers—and helped Seattle reestablish its Northwest and Cascadia superiority.

JOHN SPENCER

Walking toward Jeld-Wen Field early on Sunday morning, June 24, 2012, he didn't know if his game-day stroll would be his last as head coach of the Timbers. Earlier in the week, Timbers owner Merritt Paulson had issued an ultimatum: Win or go home. Paulson told Spencer that his squad needed to beat Seattle or he would be fired.

"I feel confident," Spencer said on that Sunday morning. "I feel confident we have the players to do the job."

Days before, however, Spencer had been wondering how his first head coaching job had reached a point of no return.

"If the game plan was to fire your head coach after 50 games with a new team, why would we have brought in so many young players?" Spencer told the *Oregonian* on June 24, 2012. "When the blueprint for the company and club is having a three-year plan and we have to sign young players and we want to be a developmental club that develops talent and possibly sells those players to a bigger league for big profits, then you tell me that we have to start winning now, the goalposts have been moved. And I didn't get the memo."

The Timbers defeated Seattle 2–1 in the game. What caused Spencer's pride in his team to grow was the Timbers' ability to hang onto a lead and close out the Sounders. The Timbers had historically struggled to maintain leads—and blown some leads—late in games during the season. When Seattle forward Eddie Johnson scored early in the second half to cut the Timbers' lead to one, many Portland fans and players wondered if they possessed the mental toughness to win the game.

"It crossed my mind," midfielder Jack Jewsbury said.

There would be no breakdown in this game, giving Spencer his first win in the rivalry.

"It's the most satisfying win of my entire career," Spencer said. "It's one of the highlights of my coaching career and one that I'll never forget."

John Spencer was the Timbers' first-ever MLS coach in 2011. *Anatoliy Lukich.*

Chapter 5
THE FANS

When the rivalry's focus shifts to the fans, the game is no longer Sounders versus Timbers. The names change to: "Flounders" versus "Portscum."

A Sounders fan proudly displays his sign before the Portland Seattle game at CenturyLink Field on October 7, 2012. *Geoffrey C. Arnold.*

Sounders versus Timbers

One rivalry started on the field in 1975, but another rivalry was developing off the field. A rivalry between the fans.

"The Portland fans are a little more raw," said Seattle assistant coach Brian Schmetzer. "Seattle fans want to be a little more gritty, but they're not there yet."

Tensions were already heated on the field during the game, and the fans decided to take matters into their own hands on July 26, 1975. A few Portland fans, celebrating the success of their team, started parading around Civic Stadium carrying a sign that read, "Soccer City Says Sink the Sounders." The Timbers fans strutted about halfway around the stadium before they were confronted by four Seattle fans who grabbed the sign, ripped it to shreds, threw the shards on the ground and stomped on them. Portland fans, seeking retaliation, stalked a trio of Seattle fans carrying a sign in support of the Sounders. The Portland fans attempted to grab the sign. Pushing and shoving ensued.

Timbers mascot "Timber Joey" (middle, with hard hat) races in to break up a fight between a Seattle fan and a Portland fan during the Seattle-Portland U.S. Open Cup game at PGE Park on July 1, 2009. *Photo courtesy of the Portland Timbers.*

For the players, the rivalry can be heated on the field, but they're usually able to put the rivalry behind them once the referee blows the final whistle to end the game. For the fans, the rivalry doesn't stop when the game ends.

Supporters of the Sounders and the Timbers really don't like each other. It is that intense dislike between the two supporter groups that adds a tremendous amount of fuel to an already burning rivalry.

"Johnny Come Lately"

One of the issues that consistently bugs Portland fans is the explosive popularity of the Seattle Sounders in their first four years of existence in MLS. The Sounders set MLS attendance records during their inaugural season in 2009 and remain the gold standard of the league when it comes to fan support. Portland fans sniff at the Sounders' attendance success and continue to question the authenticity of the Seattle fans' devotion and passion.

"When they were in the USL First Division, they had a couple thousand people come to the games," said Scott Van Swearingen, a member of the 107ist, a Timbers supporter group. "When they made the jump to MLS, if you look at the ECS section, it's three sections big, and they'll have one section participating in games. Then there's the other people, who are just kind of there and they're not doing anything."

Timbers fans waste little time pointing out the lack of support when the Sounders competed in the lower divisions and the only fans attending games were primarily family and friends.

"You talk to Seattle fans now and you hear this 'little brother–big brother' stuff. The funny thing about it is all we did was make fun of them for a decade. For years, they were our little brother. It was us and Vancouver that had the big rivalries between supporters groups. Seattle was irrelevant, they were sad," said Jeremy Wright, a member of the 107ist. "We would go up there and bring 300 people to Qwest Field in 2004 and they had less than 2,000 people in that whole stadium. We were like, 'What the hell is wrong with you? You have this great city, and no one is supporting your team!'"

Attendance at games during the Sounders' lower division days was anemic (they averaged 3,386 fans in 2008, their final year in the First Division). That's why many Timbers fans derisively call the Sounders' fans posers and fakers. They accuse the Sounders of creating a "fake" franchise bankrolled

Seattle fans wait to enter Jeld-Wen Field before the Seattle at Portland game on June 24, 2012. *Anatoliy Lukich.*

by Hollywood—comedian and game show host Drew Carey and film producer Joe Roth are co-owners—and Microsoft billionaire Paul Allen.

"When you listen to [Roth] talk about the Sounders, it's always the 'Sounders experience,'" Wright said. "I swear he thinks the Sounders are a cross between Disneyland and a movie set. He talks about the Sounders experience, but he tries to tightly control it like he would control the production of a movie. And the Sounders' fans are extras in Joe Roth's production."

The Timbers fans say they have been with their club throughout its history, through the NASL, A-League, Western League, United Soccer Leagues and now MLS. Portland fans say their passion and devotion to the club is more real, more authentic, more European-like.

"I think it's because we've always had this community-like Portland togetherness. Somehow they didn't embrace that. I don't mean to sound petty, but I really do think it came down to personalities," said Shawn Levy, a Timbers supporter. "Seattle is a more corporate town and more 'major league.' Which is to say they just don't take an interest in something until it reaches a certain point of cost or expense or credibility that comes with being major league."

Portland fans cheer and wave flags in support of the Timbers during the Seattle at Portland game on June 24, 2012. *Anatoliy Lukich.*

Members of the Timbers Army make their feelings known for an injury on the field during the Seattle at Portland game at Jeld-Wen Field on July 10, 2011. *Photo courtesy of the Portland Timbers.*

An average of 10,334 fans a game attended 15 Portland home league games in 2010, its final First Division season before joining MLS. And the Timbers averaged 9,733 fans a game for 15 home games in 2009.

Based on average attendance during the lower-division years, the Portland fans have a clear advantage over their counterparts from the north. They can rightly claim that their support has been stronger, deeper and more enduring than Seattle's support of the Sounders.

"Our support isn't based on success. It's been based on civic pride and a sense of community and belonging, as well as love of the team and the sport," Van Swearingen said. "In Seattle, it seems much more based on the results on the field. They're winning, and it's much more about the professional aspect of it.

"I feel like we were there for the sport even when it was at the lowest level you could get, but we were still there, still increasing attendance game after game."

The Timbers' slogan before they started play in MLS—"You Can't Fake This"—is a clear shot at the Sounders.

The Timbers' front office respects Seattle's attendance, but they are quick to counter with their own impressive numbers. The Timbers have sold out

Portland fans celebrate—while others cover their mouths and noses—after the Timbers score a goal during the Seattle at Portland game at Jeld-Wen Field on June 24, 2012. *Photo courtesy of the Portland Timbers.*

every game since joining the league in 2011, and their average per-game home attendance of 20,438 ranked fifth in the MLS for the 2012 season.

"Seattle is two times the size of Portland and you look at the venue size, for us to be at this point, with a city this size, is significant," said Portland owner Merritt Paulson. "We always knew that MLS would be successful in 'Soccer City, USA.' But it is one thing to say it and another thing to prove it."

"How Do You Like Me Now?"

Like a big brother who ignores his pipsqueak brother, the Seattle fans blow off what they label as shallow criticisms from the Portland fans and simply say, "Look at us now!"

The Sounders drew a franchise-record 733,441 fans to its league home games in 2012, leading the league by far. They also averaged a league-best home attendance of 43,144 a game. The 2012 attendance numbers represents the fourth consecutive season the Sounders have been the runaway leaders in MLS home attendance.

Apparently humans aren't the only ones who support the Sounders. The "Gorilla" is ready, willing and able to take on all Timbers fans as he awaits the game at Portland's Jeld-WenField on June 24, 2012. *Anatoliy Lukich.*

"Perhaps we are a little arrogant," said Keith Hodo, president of the Emerald City Supporters, a Sounders supporter group. "Are we arrogant? I think as much as anybody else is that has been successful."

The Sounders earn well-deserved praise for developing a marketing plan that has connected with the community better than they could have ever hoped. The Sounders' wildly successful campaign has helped establish soccer as a major sport in the United States, a development that would have been unthinkable ten years ago.

"I knew it was a good soccer market, just like Portland and Vancouver. This Northwest area has a great tradition, so we knew we would be successful," Seattle co-owner and general manager Adrian Hanauer said. "But it's certainly been more successful than we imagined."

Hanauer made an educated and calculated gamble that an MLS franchise would be a success despite the paltry attendance when the team was playing in the lower divisions. He had a feeling about why attendance would grow when the Sounders made the jump to the big leagues: Seattle is a big-league city.

"I've come to realize that minor-league sports in a major-league city just doesn't work. Not that Portland is a minor-league city, but it is a city that has not had all the major-league sports and in that regard, it is super hard to get any sort of attention and respect within the community as a minor-league sport," Hanauer said. "When Major League Soccer

A large contingent of Seattle fans pack a section of Jeld-Wen Field during the Seattle at Portland game on June 24, 2012. *Photo courtesy of the Portland Timbers.*

came to Seattle—partially because of the league and partially because of the way we as managers treated it in our community—it was raised to the level of the Seahawks and Mariners and the NBA. People were interested."

Part of the Sounders' success can be traced to timing. The franchise surfaced on the Seattle sports grid at the perfect time. The NBA's Seattle SuperSonics relocated to Oklahoma City, the NFL's Seattle Seahawks' dominance of the NFC West was ending, and Major League Baseball's Seattle Mariners were just beginning to hit the skids.

Those factors, combined with the Sounders' then cutting-edge marketing methods that included attracting fans through social media in 2008, allowing fans to have a real say—the ability to vote on whether to retain the general manager every four years—in business decisions and a willingness to go the extra mile in cementing their relationship with the fans laid the groundwork for the Sounders' success.

For example, when the Galaxy dominated and humiliated the Sounders 4–0 in Seattle on May 8, 2009, the front office was so embarrassed by the performance that the organization issued a credit to the season ticket holders to be validated for the 2010 season.

The percussion section of the Sounders' "Sound Wave" fires up the crowd before a game during the 2012 season. *Geoffrey C. Arnold.*

Seattle supporters light up the day with flares during the "March to the Match" before the Portland at Seattle game on October 7, 2012. *Geoffrey C. Arnold.*

"That wasn't Sounders' soccer and it was quite frankly embarrassing, humiliating, and the fans don't deserve that," Hanauer said in written statement at the time. "We want our fans committed for the long haul and we think this is the right thing to do for our fans."

The Sounders have reached the playoffs in each of their first four seasons to date, a remarkable feat for any team in any major professional sport. The team is winning under coach Sigi Schmid, and the fans pack CenturyLink Field for every game, but many MLS fans beyond Portland wonder what will happen when or if the team stops winning and starts losing.

"There's a lot of us that would say, 'I want to see what happens when they have a bad year,'" Van Swearingen said. "That will really seal the deal in terms of what happens to them."

Regardless of whether the Seattle fans are legitimate or an illusion, there is no doubt that the Sounders have set a very high standard in terms of connecting and maintaining a rabid fan base.

"Seattle has raised the bar for every new team coming into the league," former Portland head coach John Spencer said. "They're setting the bar for any team entering Major League Soccer. They've had one of the most successful launches of a new team not just in MLS, but in any major sport."

"You Are My Sunshine"

Few fans noticed team mascot Jim "Timber Jim" Serrill's abrupt mid-game departure from the stadium during the Timbers' game against the Minnesota Thunder on August 5, 2004. Serrill had learned that his daughter, Hannah, was killed in an automobile accident on Oregon Highway 18 at the age of seventeen. Hannah Serrill died after the head-on collision, leaving behind a young daughter (Keiana).

Three weeks later, a still grieving Serrill brought Keiana to the Timbers' home game against Milwaukee. Late in the game, Serrill hoisted himself and Keiana onto the roof of a then-dugout in front of the Timbers Army fans.

Serrill—who was holding Keiana in his arms—led the Army in singing the song "You Are My Sunshine," which was Hannah's favorite song to sing to Keiana. The emotional Serrill broke down in tears while singing.

"I just lost it, I let everything go at that moment," Serrill said. "I know I have a family, but it seemed like the Timbers Army became another family to me."

The Timbers' chainsaw (at left side of log) is prepared to cut another slab of wood during the Seattle-Portland game at Portland's Jeld-Wen Field on June 24, 2012. *Anatoliy Lukich.*

The somber mood dissipated and spirits were lifted when forward Fadi Afash, a 70th-minute substitute for Byron Alvarez, back-heeled a shot for a goal while Serrill and the Army were in mid-song. The game-winning goal—which pushed the Timbers past Montreal for the best record in the First Division—became known as the "Sunshine Goal" and started a tradition that continues to this day.

"It was one of these galvanizing things where people got together and said, 'How do we honor this?'" said Shawn Levy, a longtime Timbers supporter. "I think that was one of those moments when you realize as a group what sort of resources and passion we had."

Precisely at the 80th minute of every game, the Timbers Army sing "You Are My Sunshine" in honor of Timber Jim, Hannah and Keiana.

"Timber Jim is not a mascot in my mind. We have a relationship with him. I think it's partly because of the man and who he is," said Jeremy Wright, a member of the 107ist. "The love he has for the team and we have for him is a connection that goes beyond him just being a mascot."

NEW LOGO FAIL

Pulling an iconic logo into the twenty-first century would be a delicate balancing act, but one the Timbers were ready—or thought they were—to take on.

The Timbers decided to shroud the entire process in enough secrecy to make CIA operatives complain, but images of the new logo design managed to leak onto the Internet a few days before the official unveiling. Still, the Timbers were determined to maintain the mystery and unveil the new logo for maximum effect.

"We kept it veiled in secrecy," Portland owner Merritt Paulson said. "It was a little too secret."

A crowd consisting of supporters, friends of supporters, players, coaches, staff members and curious gawkers that swelled into the hundreds gathered in Director Park in downtown Portland for the super-hyped event on June 11, 2010. A video focusing on the state's lumber, logging and environmental roots and its connection to the team amped up the crowd eagerly awaiting the main event. Necks stretched as all eyes lasered in on the large covered banner attached to the arm of a crane that hung over the park.

Looking like a human prop in a Hollywood movie with a Timbers logo stamped on his forehead and "RCTID" (Rip City Til I Die) etched on the side of his skull, this Portland fan leaves no doubt where his loyalty lies. *Anatoliy Lukich.*

Members of the Timbers Army reach out and touch the slab of wood cut by Timber Joey after the goal by Kris Boyd during the Portland-Seattle game at Portland's Jeld-Wen Field on June 24, 2012. *Anatoliy Lukich.*

The new logo was unveiled, and the reaction was mixed as a smattering of boos echoed from the crowd.

"I hated the initial logo," said Garrett Dittfurth, a Timbers supporter. "It looked like a cartoon. I—and many other people—hated it."

Some fans cheered the look of the new MLS logo, but they were quickly drowned out by the growing chorus of boos from a very vocal cadre of Timbers Army fans. The boos then transformed into more nasty chant.

"You f---ed up!" Clap. Clap. Clap-Clap-Clap. "You f---ed up!" Clap. Clap. Clap-Clap-Clap."

Tempers rose faster than the decibel level.

"They were very vocal in terms of their displeasure. A couple of them wanted to confront me," Portland owner Merritt Paulson said. "They were very vocal, and they made a scene. Alcohol was probably involved."

An unhappy Paulson and an equally unhappy group of supporters confronted each other to exchange verbal jabs and insults.

"I responded testily after getting harassed by some fans. I was walking away from them, and I turned around to say something else. And Chris [Metz, the Timbers vice-president of communications] said, 'Let's keep

An unknown Timbers fan displays artistic talent in front of Jeld-Wen Field. *Photo courtesy of the Portland Timbers.*

walking,'" Paulson said. "I had been standing next to a guy who had been screaming, 'Screw Merritt Paulson! Screw Merritt Paulson!'"

The supporters called out Paulson for what they said was the owner's failure to consult them on the redesign of the logo, something near and dear to the hearts of the club's most passionate supporters.

"There's been a couple of instances where Merritt will say, 'We will not get this wrong.' The logo was one of those things where a lot of people were really nervous about the unveiling because nobody wanted it to go down like that," Dittfurth said. "The front office decided they were just going to forge ahead and not listen to other people."

Paulson said he regrets how the club handled the redesign process.

"I wished we had involved them more than we did," he said.

Cooler heads did prevail later on after another more cordial meeting occurred between Paulson and some of the supporters. Paulson agreed to make changes.

NEW NAME FAIL

The "Sounders" name dates all the way back to the team joining the NASL in 1974. The Sounders were around when the team competed in the "A-League" and in the USL First Division. But new co-owner Drew Carey and general manager Adrian Hanauer were prepared to jettison that name as the franchise transitioned to MLS.

Say what?

"I wanted to get it right," Hanauer told *Prost Amerika* in 2008. "Whether it was Sounders or it wasn't Sounders, I wanted to get it right."

So Hanauer and the staff fell back on an old standby, the "name the team" contest. And they came up with the names of "Seattle Alliance," "Seattle Republic" or "Seattle FC" for fans to vote on.

Many Sounders fans expressed shock when the three names were released. What about the Sounders? Those fans made sure Hanauer knew they weren't the least bit interested in "Alliance," "Republic" or "Seattle FC."

"We thought they were joking," said Keith Hodo, co-president of the Emerald City Supporters, a Sounders supporter group. "You look at the team names he was throwing out and it sounded like we were going to be playing a 'Star Wars' video game, not a game of football. Names like 'Alliance' and 'Republic' were the names he threw out. We were absolutely livid."

Hanauer said the new ownership wanted to move forward with the new name, not backward.

"We assumed the fans wanted to start with something fresh, have a clean break and start their own new tradition," he said. "The ownership maybe misjudged the intense passion and connection to that Sounders' tradition."

Hodo said MLS didn't want a connection to anything that reminded fans of the old, low-attendance, "who-cares-about-them" clubs of the lower divisions.

"Their biggest thing was they didn't want to tie the name to the new club they were starting. This was a new club and an MLS franchise, and they didn't want to tie that to minor-league connotations," Hodo said. "That was their justification at the time. It was plain to see that the justification didn't hold any water whatsoever."

Fueled by social media, the supporters started an underground write-in campaign to get the Sounders name on the ballot.

"We didn't feel like throwing it on the 'ballot' was the right thing to do," Hanauer said. "But we did say, 'Write in the name Sounders.'"

More than 14,500 fans voted in the four-day online election contest. Instead of choosing one of three preferred names, 50 percent of the voters

One brave Seattle fan (far right) was willing to sit among the horde of Portland fans during the Seattle-Portland game at Portland's Jeld-Wen Field on June 24, 2012. *Anatoliy Lukich.*

submitted a write-in name, and of that number, 49 percent of the write-in votes included a derivative of the name "Sounders."

The owners, worried that using just "Sounders" would be more backward-looking than moving forward, added the "FC" to give the new club a more progressive look while also acknowledging the team's connection with its history.

"We listened and heard the fans loud and clear at that point," Hanauer said. "Clearly we were wrong. We're extremely happy that our fans corrected us and sent us in the right direction."

THE COFFIN

Eyes were riveted on the coffin being carried by Timbers fans as they strutted—as if they were in a parade—around Civic Stadium on August 7, 2008. The dark green and white coffin was adorned with a yellow and green Timbers' sun emblem on top.

"One of the Timbers Army recreation teams was practicing over at Cleveland High School and a pickup truck stopped and dumped a coffin

Three Portland fans use T-shirts to uniquely describe their feelings about the Sounders before the Seattle-Portland game at Jeld-Wen Field June 24, 2012. *Anatoliy Lukich*.

nearby and drove away," said Shawn Levy, a Timbers supporter. "The guys walked over to it and looked at it, poked it with their toes before somebody had enough courage to open it. It was empty."

One supporter wanted to convert the coffin into a Soap Box Derby car, but another supporter remembered that the next Portland game would be the last Sounders-Timbers rivalry game in the USL era.

The coffin was painted with the Timbers' sun emblem and an inflatable whale placed inside. A "wake" was held, and a funeral-like procession ensued as the coffin was carried to nearby soccer watering holes such as The Bitter End and The Cheerful Bullpen. The coffin finally entered the stadium and made its way to—where else?—Section 107, ground zero of the Timbers Army contingent inside the stadium.

"It was passed down from the fans all the way from the concourse down to the dugout just above the field," Levy said.

The coffin was delivered to the top of the lower section and handed down—mosh-pit style—as it made its way down toward the field. When it finally reached the bottom of the section, the coffin was opened and an Army member pulled out the plastic orca in the blue and white colors of the First Division Sounders!

"Timber Jim said some words," Levy said. "Then the whale was brought out and summarily killed by puncture."

And that's the story of how the Timbers Army commemorated and celebrated the Sounders' move to Major League Soccer.

"MARCH TO THE MATCH" PORTLAND AT SEATTLE GAME DAY

One hour before kickoff, the lime green and blue–clad fans begin to gather at Occidental Park in downtown Seattle, about a quarter mile from CenturyLink Field on October 7, 2012. Soon, the "Sound Wave" marching band cranks up the music and an emcee is exhorting the crowd to repeat a few traditional supporter chants. The crowd moves toward the edge of the park and stands at the ready in front of Main Street.

A masked fan—that's how some of the Emerald City Supporters dress—carrying the Cascadia Cup and standing in front of the crowd wheels around and lifts the cup toward the sky as supporters roar in approval. Suddenly, the chant begins.

Seattle fans walk toward CenturyLink Field in their "March to the Match," a tradition before each home game. *Geoffrey C. Arnold.*

A Sounders supporter hoists the Cascadia Cup to lead the supporters on "March to the Match" prior to the start of the Portland at Seattle game on October 7, 2012. *Geoffrey C. Arnold.*

This Sounders fan drags a stuffed "Portscum" Timbers "fan" along on his way to the Portland at Seattle game at CenturyLink Field on October 7, 2012. *Geoffrey C. Arnold.*

A Seattle supporter uses a flare to show his support as fans end their "March to the Match" walk before the Portland at Seattle game on October 7, 2012. *Geoffrey C. Arnold.*

"Ole, Ole, Ole, Ole. Seattle Sounders, here we go! Ole, Ole, Ole, Ole. Seattle Sounders, here we go! Seattle Sounders, here we go! Clap-Clap. "Here we go!"

And they're off. Hundreds of fans, some holding scarves above their heads, others holding signs or waving flags, start their march across Main Street and down Occidental Avenue South toward CenturyLink Field minutes before kickoff. As they march their way down Occidental Avenue, they are joined by more fans during the walk.

"I think this is the biggest march ever!" one fan exclaimed. Another fan is holding a rope and dragging a life-size replica of a stuffed Portland Timbers' fan on the sidewalk.

Ahead of the march, a group of more masked supporters are holding unlit flares. They're yelling instructions to each other about synchronization and when to ignite the flares. When they reach the intersection of Occidental Avenue and South King Street, the flares are lit. The glow—and smoke—of the flares raises the level of excitement as the marchers now have CenturyLink Field in sight.

SEATTLE AT PORTLAND GAME DAY
JUNE 24, 2012

Tents, tables, chairs, sleeping bags and card games were ubiquitous surrounding Jeld-Wen Field. Four hours before game time, the crowd started lining up for a seat in the Timbers Army sections. Soon, the line that started inside the plaza located at the corner of Southwest Eighteenth and Morrison Street had snaked its way down the sidewalk adjacent to Southwest Eighteenth.

One fan walked around the stadium dragging two small stuffed orca whales—representing the Sounders—along the sidewalk. Another larger orca—the plastic blow-up type—hung from a sign affixed to the side of the stadium wall.

A lone Seattle fan, wearing his fluorescent-green X-Box 360 replica jersey, bravely walked past the Timbers throng gathered at the plaza.

"Sh--ttle fan!" one Portland fan screamed. "Prepare to get your butt kicked!"

Hearing the growing fusillade of insults and taunts, the fan stealthily widened his arc to place some distance between him and the crowd before accelerating his pace.

Above: Timbers Army fans celebrate Portland's win against Seattle at Jeld-Wen Field on June 24, 2012. *Photo courtesy of the Portland Timbers.*

Right: So how does this Seattle fan REALLY feel about the Portland Timbers? *Geoffrey C. Arnold.*

That fan was walking toward the west side of the stadium, where more friendly chants of "Seattle Sounders here we go!" Clap-clap. "Here we go." Clap-clap. "Here we go!" echoed up and down Southwest Nineteenth Avenue as fans stepped off the first of ten charter coach buses carrying Sounders supporters from Seattle arrived at the stadium. As soon as one Seattle supporter hopped off the bus, he unfurled a banner that read: "Seattle 5, Cal FC 0."

Talk about rubbing salt into a very large and very open wound.

The Sounders did smack Cal FC 5–0 in a U.S. Open Cup fourth-round game, but that score wasn't the message behind the banner. The banner was a not-so-subtle reminder of the Timbers' U.S. Open Cup loss to Cal FC, a men's AMATEUR club in May 2012. A loss that was the most humiliating and embarrassing defeat in Timbers' franchise history.

A few feet down the street, a masked Seattle supporter stood in the doorway of another bus, clutching a trophy to his chest like a newborn child.

The trophy? The Cascadia Cup, the prize for winning the fan-created competition between the MLS's three clubs in the Pacific Northwest.

Hands start slapping the windows of the bus and the chant begins.

"Seattle Sounders, here we go!" Clap-clap. "Here we go!"

Holding the cup over his head, the supporter steps off the bus and begins a triumphant walk—followed by more fans—toward the entrance.

Chapter 6
THE VILLAINS

ROGER LEVESQUE

"I'm the most hated man in Portland," Levesque said.

No question. Levesque is Public Enemy No. 1 with Portland soccer fans. Timbers fans accuse him of flipping off the fans, deliberately kicking balls at fans in the Timbers Army and generally playing dirty.

"He kicked balls into the stands and almost hurt people. His style of play—he'd play with a pugnacious style and flops a lot," said Garrett Dittfurth, a member of the 107ist, a Timbers support group. "It's stuff like that that makes you hate a player. Because guys who act like Roger Levesque is what makes people hate soccer."

If Levesque's style, goals and celebrations weren't enough, a long-held belief among Portland fans is that Levesque deliberately stepped on the head of a Portland goalkeeper during a game in 2004.

"I think that was the spark that lit the fire for the Portland fans and their feelings toward Roger," said Brian Schmetzer, who was the coach of the USL Sounders in 2004 and currently an assistant coach. "I think that just added to Portland's feelings."

Levesque adamantly denies stepping on anyone's head.

"I would never step on anyone intentionally. I don't know how that started," Levesque said. "The one [rumor] I hear a lot is when I scored a goal right down in front of fans. I was down on my knees and fist-pumping. I guess the fans were thinking I was flipping them off. That's not true, it was

Seattle forward Roger Levesque (left, No. 24) and Portland midfielder Jack Jewsbury battle for the ball during the Portland at Seattle game on May 14, 2011, at CenturyLink Field. *Photo courtesy of the Seattle Sounders.*

just a celebration. A lot these things get blown out of proportion and the stories get going."

What Levesque doesn't deny is a predilection for physical—and what Portland fans would call dirty—play.

"I've been through the battles, and I've scored some goals against them. I've gotten into a few scuffles and fallen down a few times over the years," Levesque said. "I've been around during the 'modern age' of the rivalry. The Portland fans have seen me a long time, and they're tired of seeing me."

ANDREW GREGOR

His teammates loved the gritty play. Opponents? They wanted to wrap their hands around his neck.

"He's a player that you despise when you play against him and absolutely love him when he plays for you," said Gavin Wilkinson, Portland general manager. And that's just for Gregor's play on the field.

"It was just a hatred for losing," said Preston Burpo, a former Seattle goalkeeper and Gregor's longtime friend. "Andrew had a winning mentality, and it came across in the way he played, regardless of who he played for."

No matter what team he played for, the feisty Gregor was usually at or near the top of the club lead in fouls and yellow and red cards. He led the Sounders in yellow cards in the 2002 (13) and 2003 (11) seasons and was second in 2005 and 2006. He led the Timbers in fouls (49) during the 2007 season. Opponents and opposing fans hated those fouls, but Gregor said it was all in the name of winning games.

"The majority of it was just to get a win," Gregor said. "I wanted to win so badly."

Midfielder Andrew Gregor (number 13 in white) played for the USL A-League and First Division Sounders for five seasons (1999–2000, 2002–03, 2005–06). *Photo courtesy of the Portland Timbers.*

While Gregor admits to plenty of "fouls caused" during his career, he said he never intentionally hurt any player and resents the "dirty player" label.

"People who don't understand the game completely look at me as a jerk and say I played dirty. But I never injured anyone out on the field to the point of causing any broken bones or tearing up a knee," Gregor said. "I don't think it's fair. I got a lot of yellow cards, and I had a few red cards. A majority of those yellow cards were for talking to the ref. I had a big mouth on the field."

Gregor retired from the game in 2010, but still catches grief from the fans.

"Even to this day, when I've walked into a Timbers game, I've had people swearing at me and calling me names," Gregor said. "They don't even know me."

Brad Evans

Seven words were all it took for Evans to achieve villain status among the Timbers' supporters.

"Our organization is just a cut above," Evans said two days before the Seattle at Portland game on June 24, 2012.

Evans's assessment of the two franchises was blunt but true. The Sounders have won three U.S. Open Cup championships, two USL First Division titles, two A-League titles, two APSL titles and a Western Soccer Alliance title and are two-time finalists in the NASL's Soccer Bowl.

The Timbers? Soccer Bowl finalists in 1975. That's all.

While the Sounders fans reveled in their superiority, the Timbers fans took great offense, despite knowing the reality, and voiced their opinions in the June 22, 2012 edition of *Oregon Live*.

"…You must be a cut above Montreal, too, I guess. Talk is cheap."

"The only thing Seattle has that is above Portland is their latitude on the map."

"Get back to me when you can claim this 'cut above' statement would have even been possible without the good graces of Paul Allen and his favored Seahawks franchise. Lets be real, without the backing of an NFL front office and their stadium, Sounders are just another Toronto or Philly expansion team."

FREDY MONTERO

The walk was one of the longest of his career. Staring at a sea of Portland fans giving him the "good-bye" wave in unison, Montero started his trek from the field toward the Seattle locker room.

The Sounders' star forward had received a red card from referee Ricardo Salazar, initiating his lonely journey off the field during the Sounders' 2–1 loss at Portland on June 24, 2012.

Montero's talent and diva-like personality have always drawn vitriolic comments from the Portland fans. He can be petulant and immature, particularly when he doesn't get his touches on the ball. That can be a problem for someone who doesn't always react well when the game isn't going his way.

But when Montero is on, he's a brilliant scorer and playmaker. He broke the Timbers' hearts by scoring two goals and erasing two one-goal deficits in the second half to help Seattle shock Portland 3–2 in an MLS regular season game in Portland on July 10, 2011. He scored the Sounders' lone goal in the 1–1 draw at Portland on September 15, 2012, and scored the third goal in the Sounders' 3–0 rout at Seattle on October 7, 2012.

"It doesn't matter if it's Portland or Vancouver," Montero said. "Scoring on their field is good, because they don't yell as much when you do score."

But he was arguing with the referees, jumping into the chests of Portland players and just being a nuisance on the field during the game on June 24. Montero's moves irked the Portland fans, who booed him lustily throughout the game. And they didn't forget when the two clubs met for a second time on September 15, 2012, reserving the loudest and most sustained boos when Montero's name was announced during the pre-game player introductions.

"I don't care what they're saying about me when I step on the field," Montero said.

So when Montero walked off the field—his image splashed on the stadium's gigantic video screen for extra effect—during the final moments of the game in June, the Timbers had won this particular battle.

"I got red carded, and I was out," Montero said. "That's all that mattered for them."

PRESTON BURPO

The Timbers Army's most venomous response to Burpo occurred after the goalkeeper suffered a broken jaw following a violent collision with teammate Danny Jackson in the 17th minute of the Seattle at Portland game on May 1, 2003.

"The whole side of my jaw literally dropped about a half-inch, and I've got this massive amount of blood coming out," Burpo said. "I had actually blacked out for a little bit, too."

The Army, showing no sympathy to an opponent no matter the extent of the injury, hoisted their infamous "No Pity in the Rose City" scarves while Burpo lay motionless on the field for about five minutes. Then they yelled, "You're going home in a Portland ambulance!" as he staggered off the field.

"This is actually going through my mind. As I'm walking by the Portland Timbers fans, because it happened on their side, I actually thought to myself, 'This is just perfect for Portland Timbers fodder,'" Burpo said. "I was sure I looked like some monster with my jaw halfway down on my face and blood coming out everywhere. What a freak show that was."

The fans didn't let Burpo forget the incident when he returned to play in Portland in later games.

"The Timbers fans started chanting, 'Glass jaw. Glass jaw!'" Burpo said.

Perhaps some of the Army's nastiness resulted from their claim that Burpo deliberately kicked balls into the stands, sending unsuspecting fans dodging, ducking and diving.

"He did kick balls into the Timbers Army section," said Jeremy Wright, a member of the 107ist. "He deliberately kicked balls into the stands."

Burpo admitted kicking a ball into the stands but added that he was simply having some non-threatening fun with the fans.

"Just to be funny, I kicked the ball up into the stands at halftime. Just to say, 'Hey' and I gave the fans the thumbs up and walked off the field," Burpo said. "Then I hear their fans were apparently saying I was trying to smash the ball into the crowd. What if I would've hit one of the kids in the crowd and hurt 'em? Like I was some vindictive player that hated them so bad that that's what I was trying to do."

Burpo does admit he purposely used tactics to slow down the game in an effort to earn at least a draw when the Sounders played in Portland.

"I would go get a ball from one of the ball kids. I would feel the ball and press the ball a little bit and act as if the ball was a little bit too flat. I would give the ball back to the kid, pat him on the head and walk to the next ball kid. All I was doing was killing time," Burpo said. "The next thing I know during the half, the crowd starts chanting, 'Child molester!'

"That's how it all got started."

Chapter 7
THE TRAITORS

ANDREW GREGOR

The Seattle and Portland fans never fully trusted the player who jumped back and forth between the two clubs during his eleven-year career.

"When I would go back to Seattle, they would call me Judas," Gregor said. "People said I was a hired gun and left for the money. It's funny how you get perceived by the fans."

The Portland native played five seasons in Seattle and two and a half seasons in Portland. And to complete his "traitorous" résumé, he even spent a short stint in Vancouver, earning him the distinction of being one of those rare players who played for all three Northwest clubs.

Gregor played two seasons in Seattle sandwiched between two separate stints in Portland in a span of seven seasons between 2002 and 2008. Those trips up and down Interstate 5 occurred after he played with Seattle at various times between 2000 and 2002. Gregor scored a combined 15 goals and added 13 assists in the 2002 and 2003 seasons, earning him all A-League first-team honors in each season.

Gregor joined the Timbers midway through the 2004 season. He scored 2 goals and posted 2 assists in 13 games and helped the Timbers win the regular season championship under coach Bobby Howe. Gregor scored a goal in the Timbers 2–1 win against Seattle in Game 1 of the first-round playoff series. But the Sounders bounced back to win 2–0 in Game 2 and win the 2-game, aggregate-goal series 3–2 and eliminate the Timbers.

Midfielder Andrew Gregor (number 13 in green) played for the First Division Timbers for three seasons (2004, 2007–08). *Photo courtesy of the Portland Timbers.*

The four-year starter at the University of Portland and star at Sunset High School in Beaverton then signed a contract with the Sounders in March 2005. Gregor noted his longtime friendships with Seattle players Taylor Graham, Leighton O'Brien and Roger Levesque and relationship with coach Brian Schmetzer as reasons for his return to Seattle.

"When I did play for Portland in 2004, I didn't have tons of friends on the team," Gregor said. "When I left Portland and went up to play in Seattle, I was immediately brought into the group and felt like I had been there forever."

Gregor appeared in 21 games during the season, contributing 3 goals and 5 assists as the Sounders won the USL First Division championship. One of his assists was to Roger Levesque in Seattle's 2–0 win against Portland in Game 2 of a first-round playoff series, enabling the Sounders to boot the Timbers out of the postseason for the second consecutive season on their way to winning the USL First Division championship.

"When you get on the field, pure competition takes over. It's that deep, inner drive to be successful on the field and it doesn't matter who is in your way," Gregor said. "You're going to go through them to make sure you succeed."

Accepting an offer he said he couldn't refuse, Gregor jumped back to the Timbers after the 2006 season. He wanted to earn his degree and had received a grant to pay for his tuition at the University of Portland.

"I was seeing the finish line of my career," Gregor said. "I had to finish school, and this was the perfect opportunity. I just couldn't pass on it."

The Seattle fans could've cared less about Gregor's educational goals. They saw a player join the enemy.

"I'm sure they were completely confused that I would just leave Seattle in the middle of a contract and go down and play in Portland," Gregor said. "They didn't necessarily understand, but they didn't care. To them, I was a traitor."

ROGER LEVESQUE

Portland fans rubbed their eyes in disbelief. Was that Roger Levesque—THE Roger Levesque, the most hated Sounders player—wearing OUR uniform?

There Levesque was, running onto the field in a Portland uniform as the Timbers prepared to play a friendly against Toronto in November 2007. As soon as he emerged from the locker room and stepped onto the field, Levesque looked up and saw a sign hanging in front of the Timbers Army section.

"True fans hate Levesque."

"No love lost, obviously. The hate was still there," Levesque said. "The fans were the one part that wasn't welcoming at all."

The sign and the boos for Levesque during player introductions sent Timbers owner Merritt Paulson into a tizzy.

"I was very upset. I let them know I was unhappy about the sign," Paulson said. "Look, the Army is not going to like who they're going to not like. But our job is to get the best team going, and Levesque would have been a good signing for us. When you're wearing our jersey, I think you deserve a certain amount of respect."

The Timbers fans disagreed and wanted to know why Paulson had the gall to ask Levesque—of all people—to try out. They didn't care that Levesque was a good player who had scored some big goals against the Timbers in the past. They wanted no part of him.

"Merritt was livid. He had just bought the team, and he couldn't understand," said Jeremy Wright, a member of the 107ist. "He said, 'I'm trying to get the best players in here. Why wouldn't you want me to get the best players?' I said, 'We're not Seattle.'"

Wright said he and Paulson engaged in a sometimes heated discussion about bringing Levesque to Portland.

"I told him it matters to us what type of character the players have before we cheer for them," Wright said. "Merritt's style isn't going to be, 'You're absolutely right,' because that's not Merritt, but he did get a little more of an understanding of the culture we have in Portland. Just that sign and our reaction to it was a learning experience for Merritt about how deep and how passionate we are."

Paulson said the Timbers would've signed Levesque if they were able, regardless of the Timbers Army reaction.

"To be perfectly honest with you, I don't give a shit," Paulson said. "We would've signed him if we could've signed him."

Hugo Alcaraz-Cuellar

Coming off his worst season (3 goals, 5 assists) since he joined the Timbers in 2002 (8 assists), the silky smooth midfielder was fed up with coach Chris Agnello. The two had clashed over style, philosophy and Alcaraz-Cuellar's role on the club during the meltdown season in 2006 (7–15–6, tied for last place in USL First Division). Alcaraz-Cuellar was fully prepared to leave the Timbers and move on if Agnello returned as coach and general manager.

Alcaraz-Cuellar breathed a sigh of relief when Agnello resigned.

"There was a lot of turmoil and politics," Alcaraz-Cuellar said. "When I heard he wasn't coming back, I talked to the president [of the Timbers], and he asked me if I was going to come back. I said, 'Yeah, I'm coming back.'"

Gavin Wilkinson, who was the player/assistant coach under Agnello and a teammate of Alcaraz-Cuellar, was named coach and general manager less than a week later. Good news for Alcaraz-Cuellar.

Or so he thought. Alcaraz-Cuellar said he tried to contact Wilkinson to talk about the previous season and get a read from him about the 2007 season, but he felt disrespected by the new coach/general manager.

"He didn't respond to me, and I took that as a sign that he didn't want me back. I wanted to come back, but it wasn't up to me," Alcaraz-Cuellar said. "I've talked to him once since then, but I've never asked him why he didn't want me back. And I don't know if he has ever said why he didn't want me back."

Portland mascot "Timber Joey" carries his trusty chainsaw as he walks off the field and toward the stands to rev up and entertain the fans during the Portland-Seattle game at Portland's Jeld-Wen Field on June 24, 2012. *Anatoliy Lukich.*

Wilkinson said the team didn't have the cash to keep Alcaraz-Cuellar in a Timbers jersey, and Alcaraz-Cuellar wasn't the easiest person to satisfy on and off the field.

"Hugo had a very high opinion of himself, and sometimes, he could be an absolute ass," Wilkinson said. "There were times when I wanted to just grab him and shake him up."

Seattle coach Brian Schmetzer swooped in after learning that Alcaraz-Cuellar and Wilkinson had a falling out.

"We felt we went the extra mile and showed Hugo that he was important to us," Schmetzer said. "I think he felt he wasn't getting along that well with Gavin, and he saw his time ending in Portland."

Alcaraz-Cuellar signed a contract with the Sounders on February 27, 2007. Suddenly, the Timbers all-time leader in assists, the player who led the club in assists in each of his five seasons—including leading the First Division twice—and was an all league first-team selection twice was gone, shocking his teammates.

"I couldn't believe he signed with the same team that always wanted to kill us when we played them," Portland forward Byron Alvarez said. "It was something that really hurt me. Personally, I could understand it. But soccer-wise, I will never understand it."

The change of scenery didn't affect Alcaraz-Cuellar's performance. He produced another typical season with 4 goals and a team-leading 9 assists in 27 appearances. A highlight for him occurred when he scored on a penalty kick to help knock the Timbers out of the U.S. Open Cup tournament on June 26.

Mike Fucito

He's the first player to switch sides in the rivalry during the MLS era. No one hung a "True fans hate Fucito" sign inside Jeld-Wen Field, but the five-foot-eight forward with a degree from Harvard was smart enough to address the issue less than twenty-four hours after his arrival in Portland.

"I had heard some mixed reviews about me being here. They weren't too excited that I was a Sounder," Fucito said. "It may take some time for some

Seattle center back Jhon Kennedy Hurtado climbs up the back of Portland forward Kris Boyd to head the ball away during the first half of the Seattle-Portland game at Portland's Jeld-Wen Field on June 24, 2012. *Anatoliy Lukich.*

of the fans to warm up to me. Hopefully through my play and effort, I can win them over."

Fucito played in Seattle for two seasons (2010–11) before he was traded to Montreal on February 17, 2012, and later traded to the Timbers on April 20, 2012.

His first start as a Timber occurred against Seattle on June 24, 2012.

"It was definitely a little weird at first," Fucito said. "It was my first start in a while, so I was definitely nervous, too. I just think for a rivalry game, you're a little bit more amped up."

Fucito played 66 minutes, registering two shots before being replaced by Danny Mwanga.

"That would've definitely been cool to score. I think the Timbers fans would have gone pretty nuts," Fucito said. "It would have been a little more special scoring against them. Then I would've had some real bragging rights."

BERNIE FAGAN

Serendipity, chance and fate is what brought Fagan to Portland. An English player with NASL experience, Fagan had played in Seattle (1974–75) and with the Los Angeles Aztecs (1975–77). Finally healthy after a knee injury and surgery kept him out of the game for eighteen months, Fagan had just finished playing with Detroit in the NASL Indoor League and was on his way back to Los Angeles to check on his house in 1980.

While sitting at a bar in Detroit's Metropolitan Airport, Fagan starting chatting with another customer. Fagan learned that the individual was an attorney who specialized in immigration law. Fagan told the attorney he had received his green card, which allows foreign players to live and work in the United States permanently, but added that he wasn't an official U.S. citizen.

"He said, 'I can help you become a U.S. citizen,'" Fagan said.

At the time, NASL rules required that all clubs have four players with official U.S. citizenship in the starting lineup for each game. Knowing the rule and in the process of obtaining citizenship, Fagan started contacting various clubs to set up a tryout in January 1980.

Fagan called the Timbers and learned that the club was training in Anaheim, just a short drive from his home in the South Bay area. Fagan was given the telephone number of head coach Don Megson.

"Don said, 'Why don't you come to practice tomorrow?'" Fagan said.

Training with starters such as Clyde Best, Willie Anderson, John Bain and Graham Day, Fagan said he played very well. Megson was impressed, and then Fagan dropped the clincher.

"I told them I could get my U.S. citizenship soon and they looked at me as a more valuable player. Don really wanted to get me and be one of the four [U.S.] starting lineup players," Fagan said. "Don asked me about my contract information, and I told him about this immigration lawyer in Detroit who could help move this along quickly."

Fagan returned to Detroit, met with the immigration attorney and completed the citizenship process.

"It was one of those things where everything came together so quickly," Fagan said. "It's the only reason that I'm here today in Portland."

John Bain

He wanted to stay in the Pacific Northwest. The striker from Glasgow, Scotland, was shocked when Gerry Griffin, director of communications for Louisiana-Pacific, announced during the 1982 season that the company was going to sell the Timbers.

Bain harbored hope that the franchise would remain in Portland when Griffin said that there were "two or three" seriously interested groups whom he said had pledged to keep the team in Portland. But the decision-makers at Louisiana-Pacific couldn't reach an agreement with the interested parties and decided to fold the franchise.

Bain was the Timbers' all-time leader in goals, assists and points when the Portland's NASL franchise folded after the 1982 season. The five-foot-eight midfielder said he had received interest from San Diego, Vancouver and Seattle. He opted to join the Sounders.

"I wanted to go to Seattle because it was still in the Northwest and it was a really good franchise," Bain said. "I felt it was the best option out there for me after the Timbers folded."

Hearing rumors that the Sounders—and the NASL—were also in trouble financially, Bain's productivity dropped dramatically in Seattle. Bain scored just 2 goals and had 4 assists in 24 appearances in Seattle.

The rumors about the Sounders were valid. The franchise folded after the season, and Bain moved on to the Minnesota Kickers in 1984, the final season of the NASL.

BOBBY HOWE

With his Seattle pedigree—he was a player/assistant coach from 1977 to 1983—always lurking in the shadows and having been bounced out of the playoffs by the Sounders in the previous season, Howe sometimes struggled in trying to win over the Portland fans.

When the Timbers were blown out 4–2 in Seattle and 4–0 at Vancouver in back-to-back games that completed a stretch of four losses in five games in July 2005, Howe was feeling the heat from the fans.

"Bobby should go because we've had the same style of soccer for many years now," one fan wrote online. "All the teams in the league know our style and know how to play us. We need a new strategy, and Bobby is not about changing styles."

Another fan wrote, "I do believe that Bobby is the problem regardless of what he did last year. Not all that much has changed this year except for the fact that the players definitely seem to have lost respect for their coach. I think that Bobby has rubbed some players the wrong way in his playing strategies and those players have just seemed to shut down."

The Timbers closed out the season with a 5–2–5 record and reached the playoffs for the second consecutive season and for the fourth time in Howe's five seasons in Portland. But the Timbers lost to the Sounders in the first round, extending Portland's first-round playoff futility to three consecutive seasons.

MARK BAENA

He played for Seattle in 1998 and 1999—scoring 41 goals and adding 12 assists in 49 games during that span—but never competed in the rivalry because the Timbers' franchise was dormant during his two seasons in Seattle.

Baena joined the Timbers in 2001, and when the two clubs renewed the rivalry on May 11, Baena looked across the field at PGE Park and saw plenty of his old Seattle friends.

"There was some jawing going on about me being a traitor," Baena said. "We all knew the history."

Baena scored for the "new-old" Timbers after a pass from Darren Sawatzky—who also played for the Sounders during his career—early in the game. The Timbers went on to win 2–0 in a U.S. Open Cup qualifying game in front of 12,295 fans.

Baena didn't appreciate Leighton O'Brien's hard tackle on a teammate during the game and started jawing with his off-the-field friend. The trash-talking escalated into a physical affair.

"He and I got into a bit of a scuffle on the field, and it continued into the tunnel," Baena said. "There was a reckless tackle by Leighton, and I went over and I had something to say to him.

"Shortly thereafter the whistle blew [to end the game]. And our conversation just continued. He pushed me. I pushed him. It just kind of went from there, but it was broken up pretty quickly."

Baena scored a club-leading 13 goals for the Timbers, but he considered that total a major disappointment. He had averaged 20 goals a season during his two seasons in Seattle, and he was named to the A-League's All-League first team during those seasons and was named the league's most valuable player in 1998.

Baena lays part of the blame on Portland coach Bobby Howe.

"I think he struggled to manage some of the personalities on the team," Baena said. "Bobby really struggled to find the right system or to create a system with the players he had. I very much felt Bobby had a system he was going to play, and he was going to force the players into it."

Darren Sawatzky

He was rolling in 2000.

Coming off a career season in Seattle—16 goals, 8 assists—in 2000, Sawatzky decided to join Mark Baena in Portland the following season. The duo's strong performances—Baena had scored 9 goals in 10 games and led the league in scoring before suffering an ankle injury—left them believing they would wreak havoc against opponents in 2001.

"I had opportunities to go back into MLS that year," Sawatzky said. "The deal Portland offered me was better than the deal I got from the MLS team."

The newly minted Timbers, under first-year coach Bobby Howe, finished the regular season with a 13–10–3 record, good enough for fourth place in the Western Conference of the First Division. The Timbers defeated Charlotte in a first-round playoff series but lost to Hershey in the second round.

Sawatzky said Howe struggled to manage the talent on the club.

"When he took over that team in Portland, it had been awhile since he had been a professional coach," Sawatzky said. "There was some learning curves for everyone on that team."

Darren Sawatzky (second from right) joined the Timbers during 2001, the club's first in the USL. He scored 6 goals and added 5 assists. He returned to the Sounders the following season. *Photo courtesy of the Oregonian.*

Sawatzky closed out the season with 6 goals and 5 assists, a big disappointment for him and the club. He returned to Seattle to play for Brian Schmetzer and regained his form in 2002, scoring 9 goals and adding 11 assists in 30 appearances.

Chapter 8
THE ICONS

"TIMBER JIM"

Little did he know at the time, but Jim Serrill's unusual request changed his life forever in 1978.

Trying to add a current of electricity to Timbers' NASL games, Serrill—a tree trimmer in his day job—wanted to bring a chainsaw to games to jolt fans after the home team scored a goal while honoring the Timbers' name and its Pacific Northwest roots.

"I called [then vice-president] Keith Williams and asked him if I could bring a chainsaw to the games," Serrill said. "I told him I would take the chain off to be safe."

Horrified by the image of a guy wielding a chainsaw around the stadium, Williams said thanks, but no thanks.

"He said, 'No way. It's not safe,'" Serrill said.

Serrill persisted, asking again and again. Sensing an opportunity to stage something unique, Williams and the Timbers' front office staff discovered another way to effectively use Serrill and his chainsaw to celebrate goals scored by the home club.

"He said, 'We've been thinking about cutting a slab off of a log every time they score a goal,'" Serrill said. "Williams was marketing this log product and he wanted that log on the field, so we put yellow and gold stripes around it and I would cut slices off the log."

"Timber Jim" was born.

Portland mascot "Timber Jim" Serrill hoists his trademark chainsaw to rev up the crowd during an NASL game. *Photo courtesy of the Portland Timbers.*

Wearing his trademark suspenders, logger boots, snap-back hat turned backwards and jeans or—better yet—authentic khaki logger pants, "Timber Jim" Serrill quickly transformed into an iconic mascot for the club.

Former Seattle midfielder Jimmy McAlister learned just how serious the new mascot was about supporting the Timbers after he was red-carded for throwing a punch at Jimmy Kelly.

"That Timber Jim guy followed me the whole way to the locker room with the chainsaw going," McAlister said. "I didn't know what the guy was thinking. I wondered if he was going to take a whack at me with the chainsaw. I didn't know if the guy was a total nutcase or what."

The sawing of logs after a goal and revving up a loud chainsaw around the stadium began to lose a little bit of its luster after a period of time. Serrill had to come up with some new acts to entertain the crowd throughout the game, not just after goals were scored. So Serrill started scaling a 110-foot light pole and lowering himself on a safety rope, flipping upside down before starting up the chainsaw.

"I climbed those 100-foot poles…then I wrapped my feet around the line, hung upside down and started swinging back and forth. I had my chainsaw

Portland mascot "Timber Jim" Serrill bangs his drum while standing atop an eighty-foot tree during a game. *Photo courtesy of the Portland Timbers.*

on my hip, and I fired that up," Serrill said. "That was the turning point for the crowd responding to me. I became a little bit of a cult hero at that time."

Serrill was just getting started. He started performing backflips with a soccer ball lodged between his legs on the field. He hung from the rafters of Civic Stadium and lowered himself into the crowd while beating on a large drum.

Serrill entertained crowds until the NASL Timbers folded in 1982. When the franchise returned as a lower-division club in 2001, team officials, thinking the then forty-seven-year-old Serrill wasn't interested in returning, wanted to use him as a consultant for hiring a new mascot. But Serrill wanted to come back, and management quickly agreed.

Club officials were so excited about the return of Timber Jim that they formed a search committee to find a suitable tree to reunite him with one of his most recognizable props. An eighty-foot Douglas fir tree was found, cut and installed inside the stadium.

Timber Jim was back.

"He's so unique and a real connection to our past," said Jeremy Wright, a member of the 107ist. "Timber Jim is something that goes back to the difference between Seattle and Portland. Timber Jim is something that we really value. He brought a real tangible connection."

Serrill didn't just step onto the pitch to celebrate his return to action for the Timbers' first home game of the season (against Seattle). He arrived—stylishly clad in a biker leather jacket, helmet and sunglasses—by roaring onto the field riding a motorcycle.

A little older, a little grayer and a little beefier, Serrill dusted off the suspenders, boots and chainsaw and resumed his Timber Jim antics inside the stadium.

"I had never seen someone carrying a chainsaw at a game representing a team. The first thing I wondered was whether there actually was a blade on the chainsaw," Seattle defender Taylor Graham said. "My understanding is at times there is a blade and at other times there isn't. Clearly he's got the chain on it when he's sawing the log. When he's walking by the crowd, I don't know whether he had the blade on it or not. It was a little scary."

There was Serrill, hoisting his chainsaw high in the air as it roared the familiar whine while producing the acrid but intoxicating smell of exhaust fumes that infiltrated the noses of fans throughout the stadium. The crowd cheered.

Yes, Timber Jim was back.

Kasey Keller

The sign hung from the second deck of PGE Park. "Keller: Do the Cobain!" along with the picture of a shotgun.

Seattle goalkeeper Kasey Keller played three seasons (2009–11) for the Sounders before retiring. *Photo courtesy of the Seattle Sounders.*

Keller walked out onto the field for a pre-game warmup before the Sounders' match against Portland in the U.S. Open Cup tournament match in July 2009 and was greeted with the sign.

Some people would've taken extreme offense at the sign suggesting that Keller commit suicide like Kurt Cobain, the frontman of the Seattle-based grunge band Nirvana.

Keller was more amused than offended.

"That's all part of the friendly—or not so friendly—rivalry. It gave me a good chuckle," Keller said. "It might be crossing the line a little bit. I don't look at it that way. I think sometimes we get a little too politically correct in this country. I have no problem when someone goes a little bit across the line."

Keller got the last laugh when the Sounders defeated the Timbers 2–1 in the game to advance in the U.S. Open Cup while eliminating the upstart First Division Timbers, who wanted nothing more than to show they were as good as the "haughty" Sounders, who were competing in their inaugural MLS season.

Keller was instrumental in the MLS Sounders maintaining their mastery over the Timbers in 2010. Keller stoned the penalty kicks from the Timbers'

Seattle goalkeeper Kasey Keller played for the University of Portland and for the Timbers as a semiprofessional in 1989. *Photo courtesy of the Seattle Sounders.*

Ryan Pore and Ross Smith, helping the Sounders win the U.S. Open Cup game and eliminate the Timbers for the second consecutive year.

Keller's heroics cemented his status as a sports icon in Seattle but a villain in Portland. To show their hospitality, Keller heard a cascade of boos when his face was plastered on the large video screens inside the Rose Garden during a Portland Trail Blazers NBA game he was attending in Portland in January 2011.

"When you're playing for the big rival, and you have a history in one city and then you go play for the rival in the other city, one set of rival fans aren't going to like you," Keller said. "Especially when you played for the hometown fans before going to play for the archrival."

Born in Olympia, Washington, Keller attended the University of Portland and played for the Timbers in the semiprofessional Western Soccer Alliance (WSA) in 1989, causing Portland fans to stake a claim on the goalkeeper as one of their own. That perspective only set up more disappointment for Portland fans, and that emotion would soon transform into hatred.

Keller had played in the English Premier League, Germany's Bundesliga and represented the United States in World Cup games, and his decision to return to Seattle gave the expansion franchise and the league more credibility.

"Kasey's returning home to Seattle helped launch that team in a very credible way," MLS commissioner Don Garber said. "He has been a good ambassador for our league."

Keller signed a contract with the MLS expansion Sounders in 2008 and considered retirement after the 2010 season. But with the Timbers joining MLS and the imminent renewal of the Seattle-Portland rivalry at soccer's highest level in the United States, Keller decided to stick around for one more season.

"A big reason why I wanted to play [in my] last season was to be a part of the rivalry," Keller said. "Having played for the Timbers in a semipro reincarnation in 1989 and being able to come back and finish my career with the Sounders...It's just awesome."

Keller and the Sounders were hugely disappointed after the two clubs finished in a 1–1 draw in the first-ever MLS regular season game on May 14, 2011. But the Sounders rallied from 1-goal deficits twice to defeat the Timbers 3–2 in Portland on July 10. The Sounders captured the Cascadia Cup, a tournament created by the supporters of the Sounders, Timbers and Vancouver Whitecaps in 2004.

Seattle goalkeeper Kasey Keller finished his career as the franchise leader in every goalkeeper statistic for the club. He is considered one of the greatest American soccer players in history. *Photo courtesy of the Seattle Sounders.*

"I want my fans to go home happy. I want my fans to be happy with what I did, especially against the big rivals that they dislike so much," Keller said. "Therefore, my motivation isn't necessarily as driven intrinsically for myself. But I want to beat my rival a little bit more because of what it means to my fans, not necessarily what it means to me."

The win allowed Keller to retire on top of the Cascadia rivalry.

"At some stage I wish them all the best of success, as long as they're just one place below us," Keller said after the game. "It kind of goes back to the decision of [me] playing another year of these games, and I'm just happy to have this one in the memory books."

Chapter 9
THE TIFOS

Timber Jim versus Space Needle

Plumes of green smoke rose from the North End of PGE Park as the 16,382 fans—the largest crowd in Portland modern-franchise history—witnessed Timber Jim "cut down" the Space Needle in July 2009.

"I liked that display more than some of the stuff they have done recently," said Rob Scott, director of tifos for the Emerald City Supporters, a Seattle supporter group. "I thought the 'Timber Jim' tifo had more quality than the giant one they did [in 2012]."

Minutes before the U.S. Open Cup game between the Timbers and Sounders, a very large replica of Seattle's iconic landmark popped up in front of the Timbers Army section of PGE Park. Seconds later, a large replica of the Timbers' mascot, "Timber Jim," holding his trademark chainsaw, materialized next to the Space Needle.

Timber Jim started "sawing" the Space Needle for a few seconds before the structure crashed down onto the turf.

In the background of the tifo was a banner that read: "Tonight your legend becomes history," the Timbers' response to the Sounders' tifo display that read, "Tonight, our history becomes legend" before their first MLS regular season game in 2009.

"If you talk to folks around the league, they're all like, 'The Timber Jim–Space Needle tifo was the thing that made us,'" said Jeremy Wright, a

Timber Jim "cuts down" Seattle's Space Needle in the tifo before the Seattle at Portland U.S. Open Cup game on July 1, 2009, at PGE Park. *Photo courtesy of the Portland Timbers.*

member of the 107ist. "That, I think, was when we went big time. We got respect from around the world."

The tifo wasn't the most artistic, largest or elaborate, but it was the one that ignited the competition.

"That was the best tifo I had ever seen," Portland owner Merritt Paulson said. "It really started the war."

"48 SECONDS"

If the Timbers' display marked the beginning of the "Tifo Wars," the Sounders supporters escalated the rivalry before the first MLS regular season game between the Sounders and the Timbers on May 14, 2011.

Knowing that a sold-out crowd at Qwest Field (36,593) and a national television audience would be watching, the Emerald City Supporters (ECS) knew they had to rock the soccer world with an unforgettable pre-game display.

Seattle supporters unveil the gigantic "Decades of Dominance" tifo that honored former Seattle players from the franchise's NASL, USL and MLS eras. The Tifo was unveiled before the Portland at Seattle game on May 14, 2011, at CenturyLink Field. *Photo courtesy of the Seattle Sounders.*

"We wanted to do something really amazing since it was a historic moment for our club," said Keith Hodo, co-president of ECS. "Historically, we've beaten the Timbers more often than they've beaten us. So we wanted to play off that. So we thought, 'Well, we have beaten them even all the way back to the '70s when the Sounders first started.'"

The initial displays—each sheet covering one-half of a seating section in the stadium—featured current forward Fredy Montero, along with USL First Division and A-Leagues star goalkeepers Marcus Hahnemann and Preston Burpo. The fourth and fifth displays unveiled the faces of NASL star Jimmy Gabriel and former USL coach and current assistant coach Brian Schmetzer.

"I was humbled that the fans would actually include me with Jimmy Gabriel, who was one of my mentors as a coach," Schmetzer said. "Jimmy has really done a lot for soccer, for the Sounders and the Pacific Northwest."

Next was a gigantic display of a hand crushing the Timbers' logo inside its palm. Then two more banners dropped—one on each side of the hand—that read "Decades of Dominance."

The final display sheet of the estimated twenty-six-thousand-square-foot tifo was the closer. It depicted a grinning Roger Levesque—the longtime nemesis of the Timbers and public enemy number one for Portland fans—and the words "48 seconds" inscribed underneath Levesque's mug. The 48 seconds referred to the amount of time that had elapsed in the game before Levesque scored the first goal in the Sounders' 2–1 win in the 2009 U.S. Open Cup game at Portland.

"We wanted to have one last jab at the Timbers because they loathe Roger Levesque with every fiber of their being," Hodo said. "So we thought we would throw in the 48 seconds on that banner."

"The King of Clubs"

Accepting that the Sounders is the squad possessing the most hardware and silverware, the Timbers opted to emphasize their deep and long-standing passion for the game before the two clubs met at Jeld-Wen Field on July 10, 2011.

"We always try to focus more on the team and our town," said Garrett Dittfurth, a member of the 107ist. "What we're doing is celebrating our team, our town and Cascadia—our region."

The Timbers Army unveil their "King of Clubs" tifo before the Seattle at Portland game at Jeld-Wen Field on July 10, 2011. *Photo courtesy of the Portland Timbers.*

Rob Scott, ECS tifo design director, said the Timbers don't have a choice but to emphasize their community, since they can't match the Sounders' success on the pitch.

"They've never won a championship. They can't brag about their club's record," Scott said. "They're going to fall back on what they fall back on."

Two banners that, when put together, read, "The King of Clubs" dropped from the stadium rafters above the Timbers Army sections, followed by the unveiling of the separate letters "P-T-F-C" (Portland Timbers Football Club), the rallying cry of the supporters.

Finally, a banner with the replica of a king of clubs playing card, extending from the ground to the stadium rafters, was raised.

Behind the larger display, a smaller banner that read, "Quality over Quantity" was also raised. That banner was a clear reference to the Timbers continued amusement—maybe jealousy?—at the Sounders' record-shattering attendance and the implication that many of those fans are fair-weather supporters compared to the Timbers' more passionate support.

"When we had 'Quality over Quantity,' what that was saying is that even though Seattle may have a larger attendance, our fans are true fans, ones with a real passion for their city," Wright said.

"REMEMBERING A LEGEND"

The size? Twenty-thousand square feet. The weight? Nearly a ton.

The behemoth-like tifo required twenty-two lines of rope and sixty-six riggers to hoist the banner, which blanketed nearly every section of the north end of Jeld-Wen Field.

"When I walked into the stadium and I saw all those ropes in front of their section, I thought, 'Wow, this is going to be big,'" said Rob Scott, the ECS director of tifos. "Then when it went up, it was big."

Tifo designer Eduardo Tecum knew he had a big project to complete. Once he started working on the project, he rarely stopped for breaks.

"He started one night and went for twenty-four hours straight," said Scott Van Swearingen, a member of the 107ist supporter group and project manager for the tifo. "He slept at the warehouse, and then he got back to work and finished it off."

The idea to add local legend Clive Charles surfaced during a discussion focusing on the tifo's message.

The Timbers honored Clive Charles during the unveiling of their tifo before the Seattle at Portland game at Jeld-Wen Field on June 24, 2012. *Anatoliy Lukich.*

"I said, 'I want you to inspire the current players on the field and the people in the organization to be better than anyone that's come before them.' You want them to be better than Clive. To try and reach his status," Van Swearingen said. "When they've passed away, they left an impact not only with the club, but with the community."

Tecum created the tagline, "Legends are born when the previous are surpassed," which Van Swearingen said represented the team and the city, while trying to inspire others to surpass Charles's legacy.

Wright said he needed approval from the Timbers organization to hoist the banner. Ken Puckett, the team's senior vice-president of operations, was concerned about the weight of the tifo and the stress exerted on the stadium roof.

"Ken was a little uneasy about it until we finally tested it and pulled it up there," Wright said. "The engineer said it would be fine. Once we had everything checked out, that's when we decided to go for it."

"ALL IN"

Sounders coach Sigi Schmid had a good feeling about the Sounders' chance to win before the game started on October 7, 2012.

"I was glad that I had a royal flush," Schmid said with a laugh. "I felt good about that going into the game. I thought that was important."

Schmid made the comment after he was prominently displayed on the tifo created and unveiled by the Emerald City Supporters before the Portland at Seattle game at CenturyLink Field.

The tifo started with fans in one section revealing a small banner with the word "Tonight." Another small banner revealed the words "We Go." In between those sections, a larger banner was opened, one that covered a full section and the suite boxes. On it was a poker-playing and tuxedo-wearing Schmid leaning back in a chair, holding playing cards that revealed a royal flush consisting of an ace, king, queen, jack and ten of hearts. Schmid was flanked by four masked members of the ECS.

The Sounders supporters unveil their "All In" tifo—featuring Seattle coach Sigi Schmid—before the Portland at Seattle game at CenturyLink Field on October 7, 2012. *Geoffrey C. Arnold.*

"The Timbers have used the 'King of Clubs' theme, and we thought, 'What's the best hand in poker?' A royal flush," said Scott, the ECS director of tifos. "So we gave Sigi a royal flush in the display."

Underneath were the words "All In" on the bottom of the banner. Looking closely, on the back of the card player opposite Schmid are the letters "kinson" and that player is holding a king of clubs and four other meaningless cards.

"Originally, the other card player was John Spencer. But he was fired as we were making the display," Scott said. "We hadn't painted that part of the display yet, so we just changed it."

After the game, Schmid was teary-eyed when talking about the tifo that honored him.

"It was a little bit emotional for me, but I was really proud of that," Schmid said. "This club has been the best thing that's happened to me in soccer. I'm thankful every day that I'm here."

Chapter 10
THE ODDITIES

THE SIGN

The Timbers couldn't wait until officially joining MLS in 2011 to stoke the rivalry with the Sounders. They started needling the Sounders well in advance.

With the regular season six months away, the Timbers paid for a billboard advertisement promoting the team joining MLS in September 2010. The billboard display was about a half-mile from CenturyLink Field in Seattle. The billboard read, "Portland, Oregon, Soccer City USA 2011." The Timbers' logo was also pictured on the display.

"During our prelaunch planning, we were discussing how we were going to have some fun and create some buzz," said Mike Golub, the Timbers chief operating officer. "We thought we would poke a little fun at our friends up north. Stoke the flames of a rivalry that we knew was going to be burning bright once we got into the league."

Portland fans—and some club staff members—have always questioned the authenticity of Seattle fans. They point to the team's anemic attendance when the Sounders competed in the lower divisions and then set Major League Soccer attendance records after joining MLS in 2009.

Paying to erect a billboard advertisement promoting the team deep in enemy territory was an audacious move by the Timbers.

"We put the board up and videotaped it in the stealth of the night," Golub said. "It became a viral sensation."

HONORING LEVESQUE

Normally, a celebration honoring a retired player usually occurs after some time has passed—say, a year after the player hung up his boots. However, when the retiree is Seattle legend and longtime Portland nemesis Roger Levesque, the Sounders, unable to resist getting in one last dig at the Timbers, decided the heck with protocol. Less than three months after Levesque announced his retirement in July, the Sounders honored him in a pre-game celebration before the club hosted the Timbers at CenturyLink Field on October 7, 2012.

Levesque was given a "Golden Scarf," an honor reserved for special guests. Levesque also announced the Sounders' starting 11 during pre-game introductions.

"Just being here, feeling the energy and feeding off the energy of the fans, is awesome," Levesque said. "I thought there would be some emotional moments, but I am just excited, excited to watch the guys play, and they're out there doing amazing things."

Levesque's most amazing play was his "48 seconds" goal against the Timbers in the U.S. Open Cup game at Portland in 2009. Levesque scored on a beautiful header just 48 seconds into the game that powered the Sounders to a 2–1 win. The goal was one of many goals Levesque scored against Portland during his ten-year career.

Levesque said it was a little strange to be on the field in street clothes instead of in uniform for a game against the Timbers.

"I'm thinking the Timbers Army is going to cheer, just because they're finally done with me," Levesque said. "They don't have to deal with me anymore."

"VOTE FOR ADRIAN"

Rarely are fans given enough clout to make changes to the front office personnel of a club, but Seattle fans possess the power to do just that. When the Sounders were created in 2009, co-owner/actor/game show host Drew Carey wanted to give the fans more power in the operation of the franchise. He came up with the idea of giving the club's season-ticket holders the ability to retain or fire general manager Adrian Hanauer every four years.

A minimum of ten thousand votes had to be cast before the team considered the decision valid. Hanauer would stay or go based on whether the "ayes" or "nays" reached 50.1 percent of the overall vote, a simple majority.

Giving fans the ability to fire a club executive is nearly unprecedented in professional sports in the United States, but Carey's idea surfaced after he paid a visit to Spain, where supporters of world soccer powers FC Barcelona and Real Madrid have been allowed to vote on management positions for decades.

"I thought it was the greatest idea ever. And I thought, 'I want to do this in the U.S.' We want to keep fans in the fold—the fans can strike back at us," Carey told the *New York Times* on October 3, 2012. "I'm thinking really long term, and long after we're dead, we're going to have this system where the fans aren't going to have to abandon their team. They're going to be able to vote out their general manager."

Carey pitched his idea to Joe Roth, the Sounders' majority co-owner. Carey didn't need to do much convincing before Roth was on board.

"I got calls from owners in other sports telling me I was out of my mind," Roth told the *Seattle Times* on October 4, 2012.

It's not the first time the Seattle fans have had a say in club decisions. The fans overruled management and selected the name "Sounders"—despite it not being an option on the ballot—in March 2008. Members have also voted on the name of the association ("Alliance"), band name ("Sound Wave"), Golden Scarf recipients and the scarf design for season ticket holders for the 2013 season. But a fan vote on the fate of the general manager? That was taking fan involvement to an entirely different level.

Even if he was sacked by the fans, Hanauer would continue to be involved with the club. He possesses a 32.5 percent stake in the franchise as co-owner and has presided over a club whose performance has exceeded everyone's dreams.

Four consecutive MLS playoff appearances. Three consecutive U.S. Open Cup titles (their bid for an unprecedented fourth consecutive cup title ended with a loss in the 2012 championship game). The Sounders have been the runaway leaders in attendance since joining MLS.

Still, what would happen if the "nays" were the majority?

"I flew up here with Joe Roth, and I said to him, 'Hey, what are you going to do if Adrian gets knocked out?' He said, 'We'll find a new general manager,'" MLS commissioner Don Garber said. "I looked at him to try and see if he was kidding around, and he wasn't. So they're very serious about it." Hanauer was retained after voters cast 13,271 votes to retain and 504 to remove.

#GWOUT

Like molehills surfacing in a pristine lawn, about a dozen signs popped up in the Timbers Army section at the beginning of the Timbers' home game against Vancouver on August 25, 2012.

"#GWOUT"

The sign left little doubt about what a growing number of Portland fans wanted: fire Gavin Wilkinson!

A reader comment from the August 22, 2012 edition of *Oregon Live* said, "GW is so arrogant and out of touch with reality. He acts like he has no blame for the situation the Timbers are in. Hello GW, you helped put this mess together now own up to it. Or just leave town and let Paulson hire a MLS caliber GM."

The hashtag started trending on Twitter immediately after the Timbers' 3–2 loss at New York on August 19. The Timbers had blown—again—another lead, this time a 2–0 advantage in the first half. The loss extended the Timbers' winless streak to seven games (0–5–2) after Wilkinson took over as interim coach after former head coach John Spencer was fired on July 9.

The signs appeared—along with the boos—among the fans when Wilkinson walked onto the field at the start of the game against the Whitecaps. The signs were even more prominent at halftime, when Wilkinson couldn't help but see the Timbers Army sections as he rapidly walked off the field. At that moment, Wilkinson probably wished the tunnel leading to the players' locker room wasn't located directly under the Timbers Army sections.

"I'm human," Wilkinson said. "As an individual, you can't help but feel what people have been saying about you."

Some of the fans' criticism of Wilkinson crossed the line in civility, prompting club owner Merritt Paulson to engage in a tweeting war with fans on Twitter while defending the general manager in the hours following the loss at New York.

Paulson called some of the fans—whom he labeled as a minority—"idiots" and "moronic," while cursing the group. On Twitter on August 20, 2012, he tweeted, "When we win a cup I hope the same morons starting this movement line up to kiss Gavin's ass."

Wilkinson took the high road in his responses. He acknowledged the fans' frustrations but added that he wouldn't alter his approach toward the club and said the process will take time.

"I'd much rather have fans that care. I care as much as they do," Wilkinson told the *Oregonian* on August 22, 2012. "Now I find myself in a position I don't want to be in. But I'll manage it. And if it means taking a few bullets to the end of the year to find out what we need to do to move forward, so be it."

Chapter 11
THE FUTURE

The future of the Seattle-Portland rivalry and its impact on Major League Soccer was on full display on October 7, 2012, as a packed house filled CenturyLink Field to watch the Portland at Seattle game that was broadcast nationally on ESPN.

"It's a great moment," MLS commissioner Don Garber said. "I never, ever thought I would see anything like that."

The "packed house" that Garber saw wasn't the normal 38,000-plus fans attending a Sounders game. A crowd of 66,452 jammed into the stadium for the game on a gorgeously sunny Sunday evening. The attendance represented the largest crowd in Seattle's franchise history and second-largest crowd for a stand-alone game (not part of an international double-header) in MLS history, trailing only the 69,255 fans who attended the league's inaugural match between New York and Los Angeles at the Rose Bowl on April 13, 1996.

"It's a historic moment, and I wanted to be a part of this historic moment," Garber said. "I went to the game in New York [the previous] night, and I was sitting at that game and I said, 'You know what? I've gotta go to the game in Seattle.' I hopped on a plane and came out here."

The Sounders decided earlier in the year to pull the tarp that covered the upper deck sections and open the entire stadium for four games that included the Timbers' only appearance in Seattle during the 2012 season.

"We knew we were starting with a base of thirty-nine thousand. We had a good idea we could get into the fifties, maybe into the sixties," said Adrian Hanauer, general manager and co-owner of the Sounders. "Knowing it was the one visit from Portland coming to Seattle late in the season, we had a pretty good idea that we could, if not sell out, sell into the sixties."

(Note: The record attendance for an MLS game is 92,650 on August 6, 2005, at the Los Angeles Coliseum for Chivas USA–New England as part of a double-header with Barcelona-CD Chivas Guadalajara.)

The large crowd was the fourth time that at least 55,000 fans attended a Sounders game during the 2012 season and continued the explosive growth in Seattle for the fourth consecutive season. The Sounders led the league in average attendance (43,144) and overall attendance (733,441), with both numbers setting new MLS records.

"It's just a perfect alignment of the right pent-up demand and certainly great team branding, really focused ownership, passionate and knowledgeable fans and a city that's really embraced the team from the start," Garber said. "It was really a perfect storm."

Meanwhile, the Timbers sold out every home game in 2012, extending their consecutive sellout streak to 34 games, going back to when they joined MLS in 2011. The sellouts continued as the Timbers expanded seating capacity at Jeld-Wen Field in 2012, increasing the number of seats from 18,627 during the 2011 season to 20,438 in 2012.

The two teams begin their pre-game march onto the field before the Seattle at Portland game at Jeld-Wen Field on June 24, 2012. *Anatoliy Lukich.*

"We want to build this thing to be successful for many, many years. We want to create something that will be part of Portland's sports fabric for generations," said Mike Golub, the Timbers' chief operating officer. "All of our decisions are made with an eye toward what's best for the long-term success of this club. We think we have the best soccer environment in North America."

The attendance at the Sounders and Timbers games reflected the increased interest in MLS games. Powered by the Sounders, Timbers and new or renovated stadiums in Kansas City, Montreal and Houston, average attendance increased to an all-time high of 18,807 a game during the regular season in 2012, breaking the record of 17,872 in 2011. Overall league attendance increased to an all-time high of 6,074,729 in 2012, breaking the record of 5,468,849 in 2011.

"There have been a lot of good decisions along the way, which have led to moments like this," Hanauer said. "The rivalries. The increased television exposure. The stadiums that other people have built. The quality of play improving. All of it has led to days like this. I think there are a lot more of them coming in the future."

If there is one area where improvement is needed and would likely accelerate the league's popularity, it's television ratings. With a new deal with the NBC Sports Network (NBCSN) and continuing coverage from ESPN, the league is positioned to increase its ratings.

More than 888,000 viewers watched the Seattle at Portland game that was broadcast nationally on ESPN on June 24. The game was the network's highest-rated broadcast of the 2012 season, and the number of viewers was the third-highest ever for an MLS regular season game. The second game of the series, played in Portland on September 15, was broadcast on NBC and attracted 576,000 viewers. It was the first time the over-the-air network televised an MLS game. The optics of a packed stadium—with more than 66,000 fans in CenturyLink Field in Seattle or a passionate group of fans known as the Timbers Army as part of more than 20,000 fans in Jeld-Wen Field—will help draw more viewers to MLS.

"There isn't a commissioner anywhere that doesn't wring their hands in anticipation when you have historic, legendary and storied matchups," Garber said. "That will drive ratings and helps us break through the clutter."

If MLS is to continue its growth trend, the Seattle-Portland rivalry will be the engine. The rivalry contains all the elements needed for attracting casual fan interest—big crowds, rival fans who hate each other and increasingly heated on-field competition between the two clubs.

Seattle midfielder Osvaldo Alonso (middle) yells at Portland midfielder James Marcelin (on turf) during the Seattle at Portland game at Jeld-Wen Field on July 10, 2011. *Photo courtesy of the Portland Timbers.*

The success of the Seattle-Portland rivalry—and an unbalanced schedule—was a big reason why MLS revamped its regular season schedule to promote and take advantage of regional rivalries. There were more games involving matchups such as New York–D.C. United and San Jose–Los Angeles in 2012. Not surprisingly, attendance increased.

Even when MLS expands to 20 teams and beyond in the future, it's likely the league will continue promoting regional rivalries. MLS officials hope what has happened in the Seattle-Portland rivalry can be duplicated around the league.

The recipe for success? Forty years of history; proximity of two cities; passionate, European-like supporters who love the game; and intense competition. That's what has made the Seattle-Portland rivalry what it is today:

The best in the United States.

BIBLIOGRAPHY

INTRODUCTION

Hahn, John. "Portland Soccer Success Predicted." *Oregonian*, March 24, 1975.
———. "Soccer Club Tabs Name of Timbers." *Oregonian*, March 9, 1975.
Polis, John. "Paul: Fan-player Association Key to Soccer Success." *Oregonian*, April 8, 1975.

THE GAMES

Arnold, Geoffrey C. "Seattle Sounders' Brad Evans Calls Timbers Supporters a Bunch of Drunks." OregonLive, June 22, 2012.
———. "Seattle Sounders' Brad Evans: 'Our Organization Is Just a Cut Above.'" OregonLive, June 21, 2012.
Mayers, Joshua. "Portland Earns 2–1 Victory Over Sounders." *Seattle Times*, June 24, 2012.
Polis, John. "Seattle Tips Portland, 1–0, in Wet Opener." *Oregonian*, May 2, 1975.
———. "Withe Connects for Two Goals." *Oregonian*, July 27, 1975.
Ruiz, Don. "Sounders' Skid Continues." *Tacoma News-Tribune*, June 25, 2012.

THE PLAYERS

Arnold, Geoffrey C. "MLS Combine: Does Darlington Nagbe Want to Play in Vancouver?" *Oregonian*, January 10, 2011.

Buker, Paul. "Best Signs 'Lovely' Pact with Timbers." *Oregonian*, February 13, 1979.

———. "Toronto Turns Stale Despite Best Boost." *Oregonian*, June 21, 1981.

Clark, Dave. "Roger Davies—Golden Scarf Awardee, Sounders Legend." Sounders at Heart.com, July 18, 2011.

Gaschk, Matt. "Marcus Hahnemann Joins Sounders Training." SoundersFC.com, September 17, 2012.

Robinson, Bob. "Kelly's Footwork Brands Timbers." *Oregonian*, May 3, 1975.

THE COACHES

Arace, Michael. "Unpleasant Aftermath a Case of 'He Said, He Said.'" *Columbus Dispatch*, December 11, 2008.

Fentress, Aaron. "Timbers Coach John Spencer Disappointed in Seattle's 'Excuses' Following Saturday's 1–1 Game." *Oregonian*, May 17, 2011.

Johnson, Heather. "Camelot, Seattle Style." HistoryLink.com, July 20, 2003.

Mitchell, Shawn. "Separation Anxiety—Schmid Decides to Leave after Crew Disrupts Talks with Expansion Team." *Columbus Dispatch*, December 11, 2008.

Orr, Michael. *The 1975 Portland Timbers: Birth of Soccer City USA*. Charleston, SC: The History Press, 2011.

THE FANS

Mayers, Joshua. "Sounders Talk Trash a Bit as Sunday Duel with Timbers Nears." *Seattle Times*, June 21, 2012.

ODDITIES

Mayers, Joshua. "Sounders GM Vote Just Part of Staying Connected with Fans." *Seattle Times*, October 4, 2012.

Pilon, Mary. "Rooting on the Home Team, and Voting on Its GM." *New York Times*, October 3, 2012.

ADDITIONAL RESOURCES

MLS Fact and Record Book (2012 edition)
MLS Fact and Record Book (2009 edition)
Oregonian
Portland Timbers Media Guides (1977, 1978, 1980 editions)
Portland Timbers Media Guides (2001 through 2012 editions)
Seattle Sounders Media Guide (2010 and 2011 editions)
Seattle Times
United Soccer Leagues Media Guide (2009 and 2010 editions)

WEBSITES

Daval.powweb.com
DaveLittnerspectrum.net
Fanbase.com
Goal.com
MLSSoccer.com
NASLjerseys.com
Oursportscentral.com
PortlandTimbers.com
Seattlehockey.net
Seattlepitch.tripod.com
Soccercityusa.com
SoundersFC.com
Tripod.com

INDEX

ABOUT THE AUTHOR

G eoffrey C. Arnold has been a reporter for the *Oregonian* for twenty years, including the past two years covering the Portland Timbers and Major League Soccer and a year with the USL First Division Timbers. He has covered a variety of sports and events, including the MLS Cup, NFL Super Bowl, NBA Finals and NCAA Final Four. Arnold has also written for numerous magazines, appeared on television sports shows and on sports radio.